Edgar Cayce's

BELOVED FAIRY GARDEN

by

Sandra Duggan RN, BSN

DEDICATED

to

SAI BABA

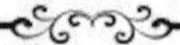

With deep love and appreciation

For all your help

THE FAIRY REALM

EDGAR CAYCE

EDGAR EVANS CAYCE

CHARLES THOMAS CAYCE

GLADYS DAVIS

KAREN JANINE DAVIS

T. J. DAVIS

BARBARA DUGGAN

CLAIRE GARDNER

JOAN GRASSER

ANDY RUSSO

JAN TIETJEN

MEGAN TIETJEN

CONTENTS

Young Edgar

Chapter One
BACKGROUND, BIRDS AND WEATHER

That is my whole purpose – if I know anything – HELP OTHERS to find the GOD in themselves. (2441-4) R13 1-4-43

BACKGROUND

Edgar Cayce is known world-wide as a psychic and medical intuitive who gave over 14,000 readings between 1901 and 1944: 9,000 on health related matters, and 212 for himself personally. He was born March 18, 1877 on a farm near Hopkinsville KY, and died January 3, 1945 at the age of 67 in Virginia Beach, VA. Edgar was a very unusual child who could talk with invisible playmates, flowers, trees, animals, birds and the Fairy Realm. Reprimands from various family members made him ashamed of these experiences, but to him they were very real. When he was 61, he dictated the following autobiographical story to his stenographer, Gladys Davis. He was nine years old when this occurred.

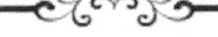

A TRUE STORY

"Come, Eddie. Don't you wish to help Auntie gather some greens for dinner? I think I saw some lovely wild mustard, as I came through the field from Uncle Jim's the other evening."

As the boy and his aunt went through the lot by the barn, where many unusual things had happened to Eddie – or so he thought, he began to speak to his aunt about them.

"Auntie, I love to play in that barn! I have just lots of fun there!"

"Fun? Fun? asked the aunt. "What is fun? You are not old enough to know what fun is, are you? What is so funny about the old barn? "

"Well," said the boy, "that is where Grandpa used to keep his tobacco, that he got so much money for. There is the old beam they used to prize tobacco with. It is fun to go there and see the pole go up and down, and hear someone cry, 'Up!

Down! Up! Down! Up! Down!' And there is a blue jay with a nest there; I saw her building it this morning. And there is one speckled egg in the nest already. I saw a wren also, looking at the horn Grandpa used to call the boys with, from the field."

"But," said the aunt, "they haven't prized tobacco there in a long time! and you never saw tobacco prized anyway, I'm sure."

"Yes I have!" said the boy. " I see Grandpa there every day when I go there to play, and besides there are a lot of little boys and girls that come there to play with me, and they can climb all over the barn and tell me what is on every pole in the barn!"

"Eddie, you shouldn't let your imagination run away with you like that! You are just imagining things! Don't you know it is wicked to tell stories?"

"What is being wicked, Auntie? I play with the children, that I know; and I see Grandpa, and he talks to me – as he has talked to the colored men who prize tobacco. What is wicked? I see it, and it is great fun for me! What is being wicked? Is that wicked, because I see them and say I see them? "

"If you saw them it would be alright," said the aunt, "but they are not there. Your grandfather has been dead for six years now, and dead people do not prize tobacco. So, to say that you do see them is wicked. I will have to speak to your mother about that."

"Oh, but Mother sees the children too!" said the boy. "She just hasn't been here when Grandpa was prizing tobacco."

"I don't believe it! and you are just a bad boy that likes to imagine things! I will speak to your mother. She must not humor you in all this tomfoolery!"

But they went on to the field and found plenty of nice wild mustard, and gathered a basket full. Coming back towards the barn the aunt asked the boy again,

"Why do you say it is fun to play in the old barn?"

"Because," said the boy, "I have so many to play with there, and Grandpa is great fun. He tells me a lot of funny stories of what happened before the war, and during the war and afterward."

"Are you sure it is your grandfather?"

"Of course it is Grandpa! I have felt his chin whiskers, and that is the way I used to tell him from Grandma when it was dark."

"You are certainly a strange child," said the aunt. "I will

have a talk with your mother. This thing must not go on, else everyone will know you have gone beside yourself. It gives me the creeps to hear you talk like that!"

"Carrie," said the aunt that evening, as the boy was out at play, "what is this Eddie says about you seeing children playing with him in the barn? There are no children that live anywhere near here! You'd better take that child to the doctor! I think he is just out of his mind! He is not normal, some way."

"But Lou, I have seen the children Eddie speaks of. They can't harm him, I am sure."

"Whose children are they?"

"I do not know. They seem very nice, and I think Eddie is having an experience such as we read of, but think can never come to us. I am praying about it, Lou, and I am sure no harm can come of it."

"But what about his saying that he sees and talks with his Grandpa. You know that is out of the question, and what will the neighbors say if they hear about all this foolishness? You need to give that boy a good thrashing, and stop all this fairy business or whatever you choose to call it!"

"Lou, I couldn't whip him for that! because he is sure he sees all this, and I have seen the children myself. It is not just imagination. I do not know what it is, but I simply can't whip him for such as that. I just wish there was some way Eddie could go to church, study his Bible, and learn what this is all about."

"Tommyrot!" said Lou. "You don't mean to tell me you think this foolishness is of God! It is more like the Devil, if you don't mind my saying so, and certainly no good can come of such a thing! You had better take the child to the doctor. They will have nothing to do with him in any church, I can assure you!"

But the aunt was married that summer and went to the eastern part of the State to live, and didn't see Eddie for several years.

The next January Eddie's mother asked him if he would like to go to Sunday School. So he began to go. The lesson was the first of Genesis, the creation, - and Eddie found it very interesting, in fact, all absorbing. He asked his father to procure a book for him that had the whole story in it. A few weeks later the Bible was procured, - the gift of a book dealer to *whom the father told the story.*

Eddie began to read, and the more he read the more sure he became that these happenings in the barn were real and not foolish. Yet, as others questioned him, the more of a recluse he became.

That year Eddie with his family moved to a little house in the edge of a wood, - one with a great variety of vegetation. There were large oaks, hickory, white oak, poplar and beech in timber wood; hazelnuts, pawpaw, and many other fruit and nut trees. Eddie became acquainted with all the beautiful dells and glades in that wood, and built himself a retreat in a very pretty spot, - a quarter of a mile from the house. There he kept his Bible, and read it every day; reading and re-reading many portions of it.

After a few months of study, one afternoon he had an experience of this nature. He had been reading of the vision of Manoah, for he loved the story of Samson. Suddenly there was a humming sound outside, and a bright light filled the little place where Eddie sat. A figure appeared all in white, bright as the noonday light, and spoke, saying:

"YOUR PRAYERS HAVE BEEN HEARD! WHAT WOULD YOU ASK OF ME, THAT I MAY GIVE IT TO YOU?"

"Just that I may be helpful to others," answered Eddie, "especially to children who are ill; and that I may love my fellow man."

The figure disappeared.

In school next day Eddie missed his lessons as usual, and had to remain to write the word "cabin" five hundred times on the blackboard. When he got home that evening his father was waiting for him. Eddie studied his lessons that evening, but seemed unable to concentrate. Around eleven o'clock he had the first experience of hearing the voice within, and it recalled the voice of the visitor of the afternoon before. It said, "Sleep, and we may help you."

Eddie asked his father to let him sleep five minutes. He slept, and at the end of the time he knew every word in that particular spelling book. [1]

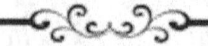

At the twelfth annual A.R.E. Congress on June 18, 1943, he again spoke of that angelic vision.

I want to tell you in my own words about my first vision,
… I had been expecting to see an angel, or hear a voice, or that something wonderful was going to happen so I had built me a little place down in the wood. The fairies had helped me, and the little folks had planted a lot of flowers and had dug a well so I wouldn't have to pack water so far, so it gave me more time to read the Book. I wanted to read it at least once for each year of my life, that was as little as I could offer. Not that I could even pronounce the words, or can yet, but I could read the Bible.
… I had asked, "Show me, Lord: do I know what I am asking for – I don't know how to ask it but just show me,"
… I had just finished reading the Book. The sun was just sinking – it wasn't behind the horizon – when suddenly I had the strangest feeling that something unusual was going to happen. I felt good - I felt lifted up, and when the Voice spoke I thought it was my mother. I turned to see but I never saw any figure like that. It was the most beautiful figure I think I ever saw, except one pretty woman - - which is another story. She said, "What do you desire? Your prayers have been heard, your alms have come up. What do you wish?" I felt dumbfounded, yet I was not afraid not nearly as afraid as I have been many years later, for I am sure I must have been much closer then than I have ever been since to a closer, more beautiful understanding of God. I didn't know what to ask for, save just as I had been reading, " As you do it unto the least of these, you do it unto me." So I said, " May I be able, then to help those who ask me for help, - whatever it may be." The beautiful figure answered, " It will be granted."
Since that day I have been the richest person in the world,…..[2]

As an adult, Edgar had the ability to lie down, go into a self induced hypnotic state and answer questions for someone who could either be present or at home anywhere in the world. With the assistance of his father, Leslie Cayce, or his wife Gertrude who presented the questions, he would provide them with   guidance. They were called readings and transcribed by his dedicated stenographer Gladys Davis.

LESLIE

GERTRUDE

GLADYS

Each person was given a number for privacy, such as (2072). (Please see Resource Guide in the Appendix to understand this system of referencing). They are currently archived at the A.R.E. (Association for Research and Enlightenment) in Virginia Beach, VA. **When referring to Edgar as a man in this book, he will be identified by his first name, and when referring to his psychic readings, he will be identified by his last name.** Gladys, who did not continue her own high school education beyond the tenth grade, expressed an admiration and respect for Edgar's abilities.

Edgar was a humble man who struggled all his life with unusual psychic
abilities that made him very unique. He may have inherited some of these
talents from his grandfather, Thomas Jefferson Cayce, who could move
objects mentally (psychokinetics) and dowse for water. A deeply religious
man, he only used his gifts on plants and animals. Thomas taught Edgar
to ride horseback and fish, and they adored each other. When he was four,
Edgar unfortunately witnessed his grandfathers death when the horse he
was riding was spooked, and he drowned in the farm pond. Edgar didn't
seem to be upset for he continued to see and talk with Thomas in the
tobacco barn. He told his aunt "that grampa could sometimes be hard to
see, that he appeared in 'beams of light' that shone from between the
rafters in the ceiling, and that if Edgar looked really hard, he could see
right through him."[3]

THOMAS JEFFERSON CAYCE circa 1840

All Edgar ever wanted to do was help people and be a channel of blessings each day. He taught Sunday school at the Presbyterian Church, led a Tuesday night bible class, and was a gifted photographer who won prizes for his portraits in the 1920's. Many of the pictures in this book were taken by him. His close relationship with Nature and God were the foundation of his life, and he consistently helped others through the readings and his correspondence of 10-20 letters a day. He wrote family, friends and others who received a reading and either thought the guidance was remarkable, requested more insight, or sought his personal counsel. In turn, he talked about many things: God, Jesus, the A.R.E., Congress, meditation, prayer, how to understand a reading or use a castor oil pack, financial worries, his health (or illness), nature, fishing, the weather, and a paragraph here and there about his garden.

> …Has been lovely here last few days, between readings I do a little piddling with a garden and my flowers, all look mighty pretty, what few have then have lake in backyard almost or comes up to backyard, so have fishing pier all that keeps me busy, when find time from my correspondence. I undertake to keep up the letters about readings and appointments, and have a bit of personal, as have four sisters, and a few cousins that let me hear from them occasionally.
>
> (1468-4) R2 4-16-38

> Do have quite a number of letters to write – and at times it is not easy, using the hunt and punch system as I do – but try and write each person that has a reading of any nature, and at times it requires several letters but I really enjoy it, just so long as there is a possibility of my saying something that will help.
>
> (1468-4) R5 5-14-38

Any incorrect spelling or grammar in his original diary entries or letters that were not dictated to Gladys or retyped by her will not be changed and are **bolded**. You will notice that he ran sentences together, started them with lower case letters and often omitted a letter in a word. For example:

> **…yes the beds about the house here are looking real pretty.and have started my vegetable garden – have Onions,peas, corn, lettuce.cabbage.all coming along nicely,been cold on them but they are looking good this morning and are drinking in the sunshine**

right along.and know will be looking real fine soon if this keeps up a while.

(464) CF 3-17-38

He had a special way with language when he said: " Listen at the birds". Edgar struggled with reading and writing and had a difficult time in school. As an adult, he read very little except the Bible which he devotedly read in its entirety every year of his life. He loved newspapers and garden catalogs, however, and enthusiastically planned his garden each winter.

We have been having some very lovely weather until this snap came along and I had begun to mull over the catalogs, in fact sent out my order yesterday for roses and this As for the garden seeds,may be early but as they usually give something of a bonus for early orders usualy try and get mine in early.

(464) CF 1-23-36

...has been fearful weather here also, and about all we could do was sit close the fire,and has it taken coal and firewood.has been a bit better last few days tho, and as I was just sitting round have been looking over the catalogs, flowers and garden. made a few selections, so you know I still have hopes
...have been looking over these seed also and getting th m lined up in my mind.

(464) CF 2-5-36

On the 200th anniversary of Washington's birthday in 1932, Spring Hill Nursery offered one free cherry tree with a $5.00 order; however Edgar decided to order three cherry trees at 35 cents each.

15

He loved all fruit trees, and one was even in his astrology chart. He was told that the symbol for his rising sign was a "...Pear Tree loaded with fruit. This is a degree charged with healing and peaceful   influences. I think this describes you well."[4]

BIRDS
Edgar loved all birds, and they loved him. On September 15, 1928, hundreds came to visit him on the telephone wires in front of his home on 35th street. Who else but Edgar would take a photograph of such an event?

In his last home on Arctic Crescent, they were nesting by his front door.

> **...We have a great many birds around us and a Mocking bird has built a nest right in front of the door, and old cat from across the way has been making it very unpleasant for her, but one of the boys I think tolled her away possibly for keeps,the young are just trying to make a get away from the nest this is the second brood this year I think for this mother bird.**
>
> **(464) CF 8-20-35**

The birds know when spring is coming and herald it with their happy song.

> **Our spring seems to have started,heard the birds all singing this morning,Jenny Wrens-Red-Wings-Mocking-birds,larks and the like,and made me feel like getting outside,but have had too much**

trouble to do muchas yet,will want to tho very soon.

(464) CF 2-14-38

Edgar especially loved canaries who brought him much joy. They are very intuitive, spiritually evolved, light in vibration, and remind us of the Angelic Realm. He built an aviary for them in his last garden and kept two in a cage in his office where they always sang throughout a reading. He also kept a parrot one summer to give its owner a much needed break.

> Oh yes, I forget the canary bird – he is sitting up here singing. I don't know whether he thinks I'm his own private property, or whether I think he is mine, from the way he acts at times. We also have a parrot, but they are rather jealous of each other. The parrot doesn't belong to us, but she and I are pretty good pals; in fact, I'm about the only one that get along with her without getting pretty badly nipped, and sometimes this - ? ps – ts – os – cis ! ! ! ???. That isn't what it is, but you know what I mean – just plain parrot fever, that keeps most of the others from getting too close.

(2457) CF 10-4-32

By 1936, he had acquired his own parrot.

> **...Has been very interesting here to see the birds flock in morning and evening for food,and of course out in the openwe have quite a number of different kinds. Speaking of the starlings, have you ever heard one of those talk, they make fine pets.wouldnt have thought it possible had not seen one,there is a Lady near Baltimore Md, who had one, she found it when very young a took car of it,now it says most any a most amusing thing some time ago I went there with some friends to see the bird, and the lady who owns it is name Nannie, and as we stood round the cage the bird said " Lawsie mercy lawsie mercy Nannie who is it that has come to see us" and about as plain as any thing you ever heard, I have a Parrot and an Canary,the Parrott is an African Parrott Gray with red tail,sh rt tail.a very good talker, and dosnt use any bad words the canary a very good singer.**

(464) CF 2-5-36

Edgar kept a diary[5] for two months in 1938 and frequently commented on the weather, birds and his garden.

17

March, 19th 1938
Beautiful day,shrubs came from Allen Nurseries, planted them.
Raspberries, Currents two Pear trees,Azalias.grape,youngs
berries, and Rhubarb,and a Willow tree.lilly bulbs.

Monday Mar. 21st 1938
First day of spring- and really seems like it too.lovely out,cut
several Hyacinths from the yard,they are beautiful, when birds
sing ,sun shines,well the whole world looks and seems
hopeful.no wonder the people of old worshipped the Sun.

Mar.25th 1938
Days have passed,not so much of neglect as like of having much
if anything to say but yesterday for the first time since coming
to the Beach in1925 have I seena Robbin make the place
something like a home,Oh yest they pass over stop and sing a
lay,but to give the appearance of making the place a home,or
singing the mate call as if preparing for a home-guess they do
not come so near the sea shore for nesting tho only a few miles
inland there are plenty-robbins are among my favorite song
birds-their early morning call is lovely-a note of sadness in the
early morning yet a happiness-not just the same in any other
unless it is the Cat bird at evening mocking birds a plenty-and
their song is lovely here-some have nested in the little tree out
front each year.hope with the willow just planted a few days
ago,some other will make their home here,saw a thrush looking
it over yesterday-also he gave forth one of his most beautiful
lays- planted my straw berries yesterday-all thebirds like them
as well as I so may or may not have a few more visitors from
them just for the berries-they like Raspberries also and have a
few of those coming on hope they all do well.
...Feeling pretty fair,bright and pretty but a cool wind,had to
order more coal this morning guess that will last until summer-
like the spring ,especially when it is pretty and bright,lovely to
look each day for a new shoot from some flower or bush putting
forth its effort to be its self,and to the glory of its
maker,appears only man puts on a show for his fellow man-to
impress them-but is that what the Robbin does when he sings
to his mate,trying to impress her with his lovely song-the study

of nature tho must be a closer study ofthe Creator,and His thought of man-do the birds imitate man ? or man imitate nature.or what is the cycle any way?.

EDGAR BY HIS WILLOW TREE, [1943]

Robins reminded him of his grandfather who had appeared near a robin's nest in the tobacco barn after his death. Whenever Edgar saw one, it gave confirmation that he was on the right path. If a robin comes into our life, it is believed that we may expect successful new growth in many areas.[6] It was a welcome message in 1938 which had been a difficult year financially, and Edgar and his family almost lost their home again.

Mar. 26th 1938
Cold,dark,rainy,dreary day,the sunshine will have to be within,it looks today

April 3rd 1938
Cool this morning,not quite so cold as was predicted by weather man,may be by night, hope dosnt kill fruit,was 42 on fron poarch this morning.guess that would be a very good record.but possibly am too dillitory about keeping it at all,

Wed, apr,27th 1938
Cool quite a stiff breeze,sun is bright-thernometer tho registers 60 worked in garden a bit, this morning-every thing there looks very nice,

April 30, 1938
Lovely day-new bird songs today-appears to be an unusual number of birds-or am I just aware of their presence,the early morning song of the-Tom-tit,the blue bird lark, cat bird,robbin,the the mocking bird,and the new ones sound like canaries-but are red,with brown , and the female yellow and black,but lovely bird-used to call them weaver bird,but havent seen any before in years and years-oh lets not forget the red-wing,he is lovely,

Sunday, May 1st 1938
Lovely may day-many roses in bloom in yard-the red one the prettiest-

Sunday-May 8th 1938
Looks sa if might rain,certainly hope it does,seems to me would be fine for the garden-had Strawberries -and peas from garden today.

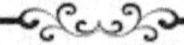

Four months later, he wrote about birds to a friend.

> …Just love scenes as you depict them – can in my imagination just see them – as well as hear the birds sing - Just love that! Like to try and tell each song, and name the bird that is singing his lay, know most of them in my own country side, and they are of a great interest to me in each new vicinity - just love them. Is interesting to me to note the ones that are familiar in all parts of the country and those peculiar to each vicinity; for instance – we never hear the Blue-Jay here nor the redhead peckerwood yet they are very familiar in almost every part of the country. But you will be thinking – I am off/on - what ever they call bird lore.
>
> (1770-3) R3 7-10-38

THE WEATHER

As every gardener knows, weather patterns can make or break a garden. Edgar did not use city water, possibly because of the expense. He planted, prayed, hoped for the best, and fretted when rain was scarce. Rain is preferable, for it brings the energy of sunlight from high altitudes and has a different vibration[7], but is unreliable. Edgar was very busy, easily distracted and frequently travelled out of town. As a result his garden didn't do well during a dry spell.

> **Rain did you say-we havent had any scarcely since Apr-and every thing is about to dry up including me.if don't have rain soon my poor little garden will perish,and has looked so nice-have had most every thing out of it that have planted.**
>
> (259) CF 6-12-39

> Well there seems to be a pretty good rain falling outside that "hopes" me up a bit – been awfully dry, my garden hasn't even come up, and planted before was in N.Y. But there has not been enough rain to make it come up since it was planted – seed – tho may be dead, don't know – possibly soon will know tho now.
>
> (1561-18) R3 5-31-41

If he wasn't commenting on his garden or nature, he was discussing the weather. The winter of 1940 was particularly difficult.

> …have had such unusual weather for this part of the country one wonders just what is happening. For the first time in the memory of

but very few, we have had ice and snow for more than a week. Our lovely lake has been a skating rink, so we have had flocks of people of all ages, sledding, skating and the like on the lake. Such has kept me quite close, for seem to be getting am afraid to be more and more a hot house plant.

(1770-4) R8 1-12-40

Cold- this is no longer where it stays warm-know it isnt like you are having-but is as cold or colder to us as yours is to you-19 was the coldest had seen it here until this year and this morning it was 12 and that is cold for hear-and to see the lake here frozen constantly for ten day had been unheard of-but is the same all over-- guess it's the Sun-Spots they have been very unusual-so have heard.

(464) CF 1-26-40

You with fog – well we had one of the deepest snows of the winter for Easter. Such a thing hasn't happened in the history of the weather bureau but some one said it happened in 1871 only other time on record. Have about 8 inches on the ground, keeps me close in as am not a lover of snow sports these days – tho remember when it would been my delight to get out in same.

(1770-4) R14 3-25-40

A year later, Mother Nature was her old self again.

Today – for the first time in many days we have a spring like day bright and sunny – there are signs everywhere of an awakening – the pussy-willow at my back window is ready to burst forth, that with the water near make a very pretty picture, for these drab places, compared to the beauty of the desert and mountains. But all by comparison, I guess very pretty here and to feel you are trying to help, gives a inner feeling of Peace.

(1770-5) R3 3-10-41

ENDNOTES

1-Cayce family papers File #3 EC reminisces Gray Box Vnsf 033 vault 1-29-39

2-Supplement to Edgar Cayce's personal file, "What Prayer Has Meant To Me" Congress 6-18-43

3-Kirkpatrick, Sidney D. *Edgar Cayce An American Prophet* p. 28

4-(778) CF 8-22-33

5-Historical Events of A.R.E. 1934-39, archives

6-Andrews, Ted *Animal Speak* p. 190

7-Gurudas *The Spiritual Properties of Herbs* p. 61

Edgar in Seashore State Park
June 1939

Chapter Two

GARDENING, EDGAR'S FLOWERING FAIRY TREES, NATURE, AND FISHING

One that fills the mind, the very being, with an expectancy of God will see His movement, His manifestation, in the wind, the sun, the earth, the flowers, the inhabitant OF the earth; (341-31) T

Edgar did not have an easy time as a child or an adult, and lived in near poverty most of his life. However, there were three things that gave him much joy and helped him through any hardships: gardening, his relationship with nature and fishing.

HIS GARDEN

Edgar's garden was such an important part of him that not only fed his family, friends, neighbors and clients – for he generously shared the harvest- but nourished him mentally, emotionally and spiritually as well.

> **We have been quite dry here, garden has suffered for want of rain, had bit tho in the last few days and it looks much better, have a good many little things of course it is all on a small scale but enough of what we have to supply the table here and often to spare thet we send to some one we feel might not be having enough.**
>
> **(464) CF 7-12-35**

He was ONE in spirit with his garden, which to him encompassed everything – the sun, wind, rain, snow, trees, flowers, vegetables, herbs, shrubs, birds, chickens, rabbits, butterflies, insects, worms and soil.

> When one sees and feels the closeness in still of the noon day - the song of the bird – the ripple of the water – the splash of the fish in the brook or river – the cry of the heron – the wave of the flower as it wafts its incense on the air; then one really lives.
> (1770-3) R5 8-16-38

He honored his plants and they thrived from his care. He would caress them as he lovingly talked with them. His son, Hugh Lynn, suspected that he gave them names but Edgar never acknowledged it.

Yes, I love to see things grow – especially fruit and vegetables. Each tree and bush seem to know me when I come about them – so they are lovely living things to me each with as much of a mission as myself. If I give them the help they respond very lovingly.

(1770-6) R3 6-15-42

His readings also spoke about the importance of the thoughts and feelings of the gardener:

…To be sure, there is a great deal in the theories that are propagated by some groups, that what is in the vegetables and fruits has much to do with the character. If the man who raises and cares for them does it with love, it makes all the difference! Don't think a grouchy man can ever raise a headed cabbage or a tomato that will agree as well as those raised by a man who laughs and tells a good joke, though it may be smutty!

(470-35) T

Feelings of joy and love can attune one more deeply to a plant and loving them makes them grow stronger and larger.[1] That is just what happened for Edgar. He had the best garden around - the biggest fruits and vegetables, the earliest peas - and Gladys said: "In all the years I knew him in Virginia Beach he was an expert gardener, raising vegetables, fruits and flowers that were outstanding as compared to others in the vicinity."[2] He did not use mulch, but cultivated and weeded with a hoe.

EDGAR HOEING, June 1936

His youngest son Edgar Evans reminisced in a letter to the author on August 25, 2007:

Dad did love to work in a garden. We had gardens at every house we lived in (four) in Virginia Beach. He planted the usual garden vegetables, carrots, tomatoes, etc. He also planted fruit trees and rose bushes and plants like blackberries and strawberries. Hugh Lynn and I never shared his love of working in a garden though we did enjoy the fishing trips. We left a trail of fruit trees and rose bushes at all of the houses we lived in. Besides fishing I guess he liked working in a garden as much as anything and some of his psychic ability may have slipped over into everyday life as I never saw him return from a fishing trip or a visit to his garden without a load of fish or a handful of vegetables.

The readings suggest that we cultivate a garden and raise our own food. In 1940, (2345) was concerned about providing for his family, and (470) was told how to make compost using chicken manure. No wonder Edgar had such a bountiful garden.

(Q) Would the ownership of a farm of approximately 100 acres protect the future security of my family and self, and if so in what section of the country should I purchase this farm?
(A) In the section where you reside! This should be the aim, the desire of every soul; to be at least to some extent SELF-sustaining; or owning and creating that as ye consume – from GOD'S storehouse and soil! Own such.

(2345-1) T

If there is to be insured the producing of the character of fertilization needed, or the making of the proper fertilizer, - none exceeds, of course, the value of chicken fertilizer, especially for some vegetables. Hence this should be used in rather an abundance, not excessively but in large measures; as well as that produced by the methods of adding such as lime and potash with portions of the soil, or portions of vegetable matter or refuse of vines or grasses in certain characters of vegetation, - but always mixed with the droppings of the chicken, - for this is the better of ANY that may be had for vegetables!
...Consider the days of old, - these are not foolish! When there were the families that produced upon the farm, how much better not only were the lives of those individuals but the character of the product –

and there were not half so many pests to deal with!

(470-35) T

Edgar liked to go without shoes and dig in the dirt, for "...am a little farmer boy at heart-"[3]

> Ah - back to nature. Aren't we all just like that at some time that is why I like the place round here - like to get my bare feet on the ground occasionally.
>
> (1468-4) R20 3-31-39

People recognized this in him and were constantly giving him flowers, bulbs and cuttings.

> I love flowers, and some of these times when you are pulling up some of those that have gotten away from you, and you feel that you could send them, put them in a little bundle and send them down to me – I'll find a place for them, and assure you I'll take good care of them.
>
> (464-12) R23 10-21-32

> ...In our present surroundings I am not yet able financially to prepare such, and the lay of the land doesn't lend itself to that purpose; but you may know, from a little of this, how much I appreciate the bulbs and flowers you sent a few weeks ago. I hope that the love and care I'll be able to give them will, at least, show THEM my appreciation; and some day I may be able to present to you a blossom from some of these.
>
> (464-12) R27 12-1-32

One lady invited him to come see her garden, for she wanted her roses to meet him! Plants and flowers always responded with a living awareness to Edgars loving presence.

> The other day I had a little experience I'll tell you about. A lady came out and brought me quite a number of little plants. The lady with her said she was rather envious of them, as she thought her friend was fixing them for her, but after she came and had her reading she felt she knew exactly why the friend had brought them to me – she knew why those plants and shrubs looked like they really enjoyed me handling them.
>
> (464-12) R31 3-8-33

Nature recognizes those who respect and honor it. Every seed was planted with prayer, and as one reading said: "And don't forget, - you may sow the seed; God alone gives the increase."[4] He even prayed when using commercial compost which was more natural in his day. He loved and praised everything that grew and did not see things just as food. As a result, with the cooperation of nature and the fairies, there were very few insects and his garden was blessed.

Edward L. Gardner writes, "...the fairy life will not come out from the shrubs and plants unless the human visitor is of a sympathetic quality. Such a visitor needs to be not merely sympathetic in mentality, for that is of little use; he must have a warm emotional sympathy, child-like in its innocence simplicity."[5] That is the perfect description of Edgar who chose some very interesting flowers and trees.

EDGAR'S FLOWERING FAIRY TREES
"...every tree can be a doorway to the Faerie Realm or to other spirit dimensions. In fact, one of the safest ways to open to spirit guides and to stimulate greater contact is through work with the trees."[6] He especially loved those that flowered, and wrote Mrs. (464) in 1940.

> Trees are beautiful-takes many of them long time to grow,we had none here when we cam and have tried to put out some with very little sucess,but have a few growing now, Willow does the best I guess but have two willows-a silver popular that have gotten started pretty well.couple of peach and two pear,they are doing very well,like fruit trees for shade beauty as well as occasionally some fruit-one of the peach had fruit last year and was nice-has quite a bit on it again this year if the salt air dosnt ruin them before they get ripe,then have a Chinese Rose tree it was very pretty this year-dont know just how big it grows-and a Jap Cherry had only a few blooms this year-a crabb apple and a maple that has started very nicely, a Haw that seems to be living. so if all these do grow might some day have the back and side yard looking very nice.
>
> **(464) DF 6-10-40**

Two years later, he was still planting trees and feeling his age (64).

> **...have been so busy trying to get something of a garden in,have neglected my letters abit-**
> **...planted several trees fruit-Peaches,Cherries ,Pears Apples and several nut trees,don't know as they will live,but if they do will be fine, like their blossoms as well as the shade and fruit-if any will take a few years to have them,but will be fine for some one am sure if they live.**
> **...think I over did it so am having to rest today,hope to be able to finish my job tomorrow grubbing ground that has never been cultivated is not an easy task however and that is what have been trying to do-set out a lot of trees yesterday-that was what got the best of me.**

> **(585) CF 4-15-42**

ALMOND TREE

The almond tree is related to the peach tree and is the first to blossom in springtime. Although Edgar planted them at his home and the hospital, they are not native to Virginia Beach and did not grow well in that climate, even for him. The nut is alkaline, low in fat and high in fiber, calcium and phosphorus, and the readings recommended 2-3 raw almonds a day for a very important reason.

> And, just as indicated in other suggestions, - those who would eat two to three almonds each day need never fear cancer.

> (1158-31) T

…Other characters of nuts are well, though especially almonds are good and if an almond is taken each day, and kept up, you'll never have accumulations of tumors or such conditions through the body. An almond a day is much more in accord with keeping the doctor away, especially certain types of doctors, than apples. For the apple was the fall, not almond – for the almond blossomed when everything else died. Remember this is life!

(3180-3) T

The daughter of (5009) gave a testimonial about her mother's colon cancer, polyps and almonds.

"In July 1957, my mother was operated on for a malignant mass in the intestines. The surgeon removed a segment of bowel to which was attached a polyp, as well as the mass. He told my brother and me that he would have liked to have removed also a further segment on which two or three more polyps (benign of course) were located but he feared she could not have stood that much nerve shock. He said he wished to watch closely by X-ray the polyps every 3 months. Subsequently, I urged mother – as soon as she was out of the hospital – to eat several raw almonds a day – whether she believed in them or not (and although she tends to discount and negate a lot she was scared enough to heed me!) In 3 months the X-ray picture showed the remaining polyps 'somewhat smaller' – the doctor reported. In another 3 months the doctor said he couldn't discern ANY polyps at all in the X-ray picture and was so pleased that he changed her periodic X-ray pictures from every 3 months to every 6 months. In another year – he changed to X-ray photos only once yearly. It has almost been 3 ½ years now since her surgery and there has been no return of any trouble or of any polyps and her last X-ray photos were of her entire body–torso as well as abdominal region. So, this is a good report for 'the Almond'."

(5009-1) R12 11-5-60

APPLE TREE
Apple trees have had a long association with the Fairy Realm, and their spring time blossoming draws many fairies. The readings often suggested a cleanse by eating sheep-nose apples (such as Delicious or Jonathan) for three days.[7] Cayce did not agree with the saying 'an apple a day keeps the doctor away'. He suggested they be cooked for most people cannot digest and assimilate raw apples. They should only be eaten raw on the three day apple diet.

CHERRY TREE

The cherry tree is associated with new awakenings of faith and trust on high levels,[8] and has fewer diseases than any other fruit tree. Edgar chose the Japanese Flowering Cherry (also called the Rose Flowering Cherry) for his garden. The city of Tokyo gave 3,020 saplings of this variety as a gift of friendship to the city of Washington D.C. in 1912 to beautify the Jefferson Memorial Tidal Basin. Wild cherry trees were already around his last home when he moved in. The readings recommended wild cherry bark 312 times for respiratory and digestive problems, and emphasized that it be harvested only from the north side of the tree.

FIG TREE

Edgar's love for almond and fig trees came from his Egyptian incarnation. He planted fig trees at the hospital and Arctic Crescent, and made gourmet fig jam. The fig is native to Virginia Beach and thrives in sandy soil, especially if compost is added yearly. It can grow up to twenty feet tall and produce two crops a year. It must be very special, for Buddha sat under one and attained enlightenment.

> Yes, our figs here are just beginning to get ripe. We are favored, in this district, with several different kinds of figs. I may have told you about this. There are quite a few little sweet golden figs, much like you have in Alabama. Then there are the larger white figs and blue figs whose season lasts much longer – and these, we have found, make the better preserves.
>
> (2457) CF 8-10-33

On December 2, 1937, Edgar dreamed that an Egyptian mummy sat up and requested dates, figs and corn meal. It is almost a spiritual food that is especially strengthening for the young and elderly, and can be eaten warm or cold for breakfast or supper. Its laxative effect would have been helpful for the hospital patients, and it was named "Mummy Food".

MUMMY FOOD [9]
½ cup chopped pitted dates
½ cup chopped dried black figs
1 ½ cups water
1 rounded tbsp. cornmeal

Cook over low heat, stirring frequently, for ten minutes or longer.
Serve with milk or cream. Serves 2-4

HAWTHORN TREE
Often called Haw, it is known as the May Tree in Europe for it is part of their May Day celebrations. It is sacred to the fairies and lives a very, very long time. Each blossom produces a brilliant red fruit that is used as a heart tonic.

PEACH TREE
Peach trees were especially loved by Edgar, for his grandfather had planted them, and his grandmother asked him to pick one for her when she was dying. In the introduction of Sidney Kirkpatrick's book,[10] Edgar gave a reading for a three month old ill infant, then immediately went to the orchard to scrape the bark of a peach tree so his aunt could make the hot, healing poultice that was recommended.

> B2. GD's note: There is no copy on file of this reading. I also heard Mrs. [760] tell of a reading that saved [1005]'s life when he was 3 months old, but there is no copy of that reading on file either. He was having convulsions regularly every 20 minutes. Doctors had given up hope. The reading recommended an over dose of belladonna, which in a few minutes relaxed the baby so that he went to sleep. An antidote had been given in the reading to counteract the belladonna poison, a peach-tree poultice, made from the tenderest branches into a brew. Towels were dipped in this and wrapped continuously around the baby. He awoke hours later and was alright.
>
> (1005-1) B2 8-8-24

A 38 year old woman with back pain, inflammation and congestion of the fallopian tubes was told to use a peach leaf poultice along with other remedies.

> Do apply over the pubic centers a poultice of peach tree leaves made in the form of a stupe; that is, get green leaves and put them in hot water, and put between two clothes; not necessarily large cloths, for the area is just that above or over the pubic center, the very low portion of the abdomen. This is to aid in eliminating the inflammation which will be relieved from the body through the activity of the kidneys and bladder. Do this every day for at least five days.
>
> (5136-) T

The 1932 Spring Hill catalog caught Edgar's eye and captured his pocketbook with the following description of the elberta peach: buy one for 30 cents and get one for 1 cent.

The nature and quality of the Peach is so well and universally known that it needs no word of introduction or commendation from us. Its importance as one of the necessary luxuries of the home is keenly felt by every family and was never more emphasized than at present when the scarcity and high prices put it beyond the reach of every one, who does not have
his own trees.

WILLOW TREE

The willow is a magical, healing tree with a long association with the Fairy Realm. It flowers from March to June, and its wood makes one of the best dowsing rods. Edgar planted one in his backyard near the pier which was an important gathering place for A.R.E. Congress and visitors.

GERTRUDE AND EDGAR BY THE WILLOW TREE, June 1941

People often wanted to know what their personal flower and tree was. In 1934, a 16 year old girl asked:

(Q) What is the entity's tree and flower?
(A) The flower is the snowdrop, for its purity, for its struggling with the chilling blast and yet carrying within it the heart of the summer light in the spirit of its beauty and freshness. The tree is that WE call in this land the dogwood, yet in that particular land it bore quite a different blossom. Just as the white and the pink make for the harmonies of the colors in the entity's experience, so do these in their

activity represent the activity of the entity.

Some may ask, from what source – WHY is it given to this entity or to another for some particular tree or flower to be its tree or flower? Because their lives, in the use of same in the period of its development, that meant the most to others, are represented or presented by that flower or tree represents in the experience of those that have looked into the heart of the flower, or that have harkened to the position the tree occupies among its fellows; for do they not speak one to another in their manifestations of the spirit they represent to fulfil a place in the experience of the sons of men? If they will but harken to the voices even from nature, as represented in the flower or the tree;...

(276-6) T

Edgar never asked what his flower or tree was – they were ALL such a living, breathing part of him.

NATURE
I love all nature, for there seems to be – as it did when I was a child – the attempt to speak to me very often of my Maker. Life in all its essence must be from that Creative Energy we have called God. Plants, animals and everything, including human beings, show their appreciation of every effort man makes towards setting forth that love that must have been expressed when God brought them all into existence.

(254-63) R3 10-21-32

(5747) wanted to teach a child about God.

(Q) How is the best way to explain God to a child under twelve years of age?
(A) In nature. As the unfolding of that that is seen ABOUT the child itself, whether in the grasses, the flowers, the birds, or what; for each are an expression of the Creative Energies in its activity, and the sooner EVERY SOUL would learn that they themselves are a portion of everything about same, with the ability within self to make one's self one WITH that that brought ALL into being, the change is as that of service in its NATURALNESS.

(5747-1) T

After he moved to Virginia Beach, Edgar quickly came to love the sunrises and sunsets.

I wish I had the ability to tell you what an autumn is like on the coast. Having spent the greater part of my PRESENT EARTHLY EXISTENCE inland, I had often dreamed of what an autumn would be along the sea. I had the experience of two autumns on the west Texas plains, another in the mountains or the uplift in central Texas, many in the lowlands of Alabama and a great many in the foothills of Kentucky – but for beauty I don't think that any surpass those near the coast. The beauty in the sunset is not surpassed anywhere, and the glory of the sunrise from the watery bed CAN'T be surpassed! While often the waters look cold, and as the billows rise and surge inland one thinks of the mighty power that drives it on, and is made to feel and know that God RULES, and all is well! Man in all his majesty can never paint nor sing the glories or the beauties of one of those sunsets. Neither can he inspire one as does the surge of the mighty sea. No, it doesn't impress one as being uncongenial – rather the impression of its power and impelling force, making man feel little and knowing that he is dependent upon Him whom the very winds and sea obey.

(849-1) R12 11-10-27

VIRGINIA BEACH SUNRISE
[photo by Edgar?]

One of his favorite places to walk was on the beach where he discovered quite a surprise one day.

We had quite a storm over the week-end, with considerable damage done to the walkway along the beach; one of the highest seas they have ever had at this place. While the walk itself didn't fold up, much of the under girding did and took out the supports. It didn't drop down, for the pinions run pretty well into the ground on the piling, but it certainly took every bit of sand off the beach. It is quite evident that at one time this shore line was very much more of a tropical region than at present; not unlikely that many of the tracks we can see in the clay were made by elephants, lions, maybe tigers, hippopatumuses and all those things. Today it is very fair, has turned warm again, and is just fine.

(849-10) R3 12-1-32

He also loved to walk in Seashore State Park (renamed First Landing State Park in 1995), his 'wild garden' of 2,888 acres that opened in 1936 in the north end of Virginia Beach. His readings often said we are surrounded by the presence of God in nature - whether it be the wilderness, a garden or backyard - where we should listen, admire and be respectful.

As there is the music of the spheres, there is indeed the music of the growing things in nature. There is then the music of NATURE itself! There is the music of the growth of the rose, of EVERY plant that bears color, of every one that opens its blossom for the edification, for the sanctification even of the environs thereabout!

(949-12) T

Ye love nature, and the things that partake of same; the out of doors, the blossom of the rose, and the sunset, the fall of the water. ALL of these bring to thee the voice of that which has ALMOST persuaded thee as to how close He is to thee.

(1809-1) T

…Listen at the birds. Watch the blush of the rose. Listen at the life rising in the tree. These serve their Maker - Through what? That psychic force, that IS Life itself, in their respective sphere – that were put for the service of man. Learn thine lesson, O Man, from that about thee.

(364-10) T

In the fall of 1932, he wrote (259).

We are having most glorious weather here now; in fact, we have been having all Fall. We have had one frost, but what little flowers we were able to straggle along with us as we moved so much last year are doing their level best to shed some of their beauty, and to give expression of their concept of their Maker. O that we would all do just that, and – as we view nature – take a lesson from that we see about us, knowing that each flower, each shrub, each blade of grass as it lifts its head, is trying to express to man (who is the wayward creature of all earth) something of the glory it feels in its Maker, presenting the very best it can under whatever circumstance or environ it finds itself; raising no hullabaloo because times are hard or conditions bad, but doing the best it can with what it has.

(259) CF 11-17-32

Flower Newhouse says "...nature is one of the most direct and powerful ways for us to experience God."[11] When we are in nature we should be humble with a sense of wonder "...that fine tunes our faculties for inner perception – namely, receptivity to intuitions, impressions and, ultimately, the presence of God."[12] His "...handwriting can be seen in trees, rocks, gnarled pieces of wood and other message-laden natural objects."[13] The readings often spoke of God's purpose and our soul's purpose.

...But, as God's purpose is to GLORIFY the individual man (or soul) in the earth, so the highest purpose of an individual soul or entity is to glorify the Creative Energy or God in the earth. Should the Maker use a gnome, a fairy, an angel, a developing entity FOR a guide, alright – for a specific direction; for He hath given His angels charge concerning thee, and THY god, thy face, is ever before the Throne of the Infinite.

(338-3) T

FISHING

Edgar loved living by the lake, and his garden included the pier in his backyard. It was hot in the sun, so he cleverly built a deep planter box filled with rich soil that held a willow tree with petunias around the base. It floated on a raft that could be moved to keep him in the shade. Gladys once said the tree had no business living – it only lived because of Edgar's love.

FLOATING TREE, August 1939

The readings warned about the harmful rays of the sun.

> Let there be not too much activity in the middle of the day, or of the sunshine. The early mornings and the late afternoons are the more preferable times. For the sun during the period between eleven or eleven-thirty and two o'clock carries too GREAT a quantity of the actinic rays that make for destructive forces to the superficial circulation…
>
> (934-2) T

Edgar's astrological sign was Pisces – two fish swimming in opposite directions. He was an adept fisherman and loved to fish even in the rain and snow. It not only put food on the table but was a quiet time for meditation.

> Possibly should not be so heartless as to catch the poor fish – but it is one of the real interest in my life, to fish – suppose justify myself, in that HE loved many of those that were engaged in fishing as a livelihood, and I have used many occasions as periods of meditation with wonderful results – and too one of the real experience of my life, when I talked face to face with The Master, He spoke of sending me fishing.
>
> (1468-4) R5 5-14-38

At his last home on Lake Holly, he built a pen in the water where he kept any fish he caught and fed them until they were ready to be eaten. He also used meal as bait to lure them into the pen.

> **…want spring to come tho now want to get out Fishing- well fish right here in my back yard-day before yesterday got 78 of the nicest perch you nearly ever saw-the 78 weighed a bit better than 20 pounds so were nice eating fish-then go in the ocean and Bay when a bit warmer.**
>
> **(464) CF 2-23-39**

EDGAR ON HIS PIER

A BIG ONE, [1942]

ENDNOTES

1-Gurudas p. 84

2-(3-29-73) GDT to HLC: "Hurried list of ways in which I witnessed creativity in the man Edgar Cayce, in
  his conscious daily life:" Historical Events of A.R.E. 1933

3-(1468-4) R8 6-23-38

4-(1797-3) T

5-Tompkins, Peter *The Secret Life of Nature* p. 9 (Edward L. Gardner was president of the Blavatsky
  Lodge, a leading branch of the British Theosophical Society)

6-Andrews, Ted *Nature Speak* p. 230

7-Duggan, Sandra RN,BS *Edgar's Guide to Colon Care* p. 81-88

8-Andrews p. 262

9-Reilly, Harold J. and Brod, Ruth Nagy *The Edgar Cayce Handbook for Health Through Drugless Therapy*
  P. 91

10-Kirkpatrick p. 7

11-Newhouse, Flower A. *Angels of Nature* p. 113

12-Ibid p. 116

13-Ibid p. 121

HOME OF EDGAR'S PARENTS
HOPKINSVILLE, KY
May 1903

Chapter Three

FIRST GARDEN, FAIRIES, ELVES AND "LITTLE PEOPLE"
1877-1891 Hopkinsville, Kentucky

For odors ARE necessary, else would they have been given to the rose,
to the violet, to the lilac, to the clover, to those things that
show the beauty of a loving heavenly Father! (1402-1) T

Edgar's love for gardening came from his mothers' vegetable and flower gardens where he spent many hours playing as a child.

Yes, I too have always enjoyed a garden. I do not know hardly from what angle I have acquired this, or whether it is something I have carried over from some other experience, but I remember so distinctly the garden at my mother's old home place when I was a very small child. My mother's father was one of the first settlers in southwestern Kentucky; had a fine old place, and the old-fashioned garden, with all the old-fashioned flowers, was known throughout that part of the country. Your mentioning your mother destroying bleeding hearts calls to my mind what beautiful bunches of these grew in that garden, with a large bunch of striped grass, some very old peonies, all kinds of buttercups, and the like; a gorgeous bed of sweet violets, and all those old flowers. It was here that often in my early childhood I met and played with those that others could never see. It was here that I was often called the strange, strange child. I remember getting a very sound thrashing once for tearing up a Hop bed, the only one that I ever saw? Why? It seemed I was directed, as I remember, by those with whom I played; but that was a very poor excuse to my elders at the time. It was the only thing, vine or flower, that I remember of ever having destroyed.

...My mother was English, of the original stock of Major Castle. It may be that through some heredity influence I have obtained this love for the old-fashioned gardens, with walks running through them, vines, trellises of roses, and the like.

(464-12) R27 12-1-32

I hope that Aunt Mary is keeping well. I know how she likes to potter around with the flowers. I'll never forget how it used to be in the old days, how beautiful the walk was in the garden and the pit in the corner of the yard. I guess all has changed around there so much that it doesn't look the same. One of the first remembrances in my whole life is that old home place,…

(4324-1) R4 6-16-26

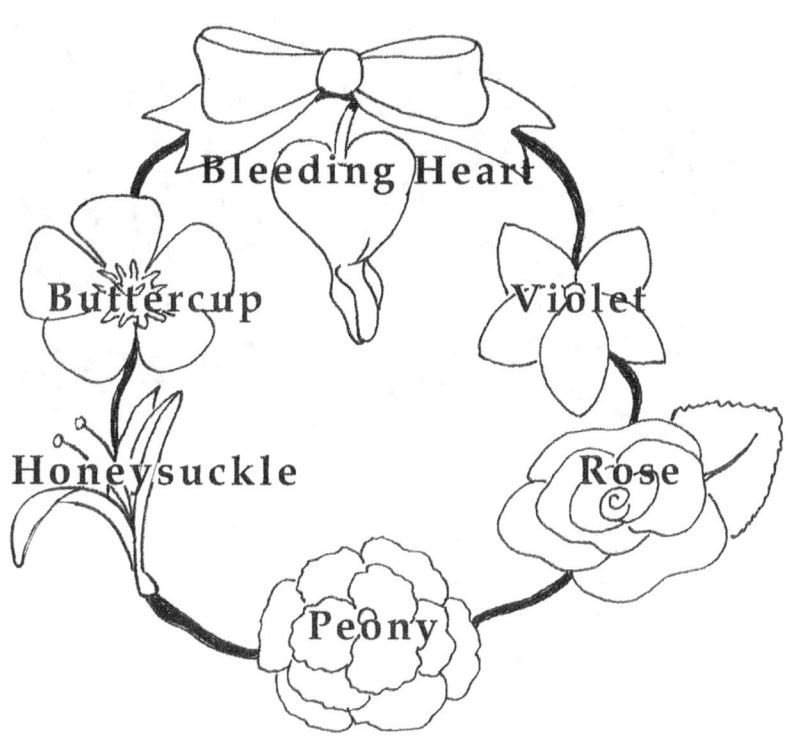

The "old-fashioned" or grandmothers garden was actually a new style incorporated into gardens in the late nineteenth century. The charm of those old gardens was in their wealth and tangle of bloom… The spirit of those gardens came from the hands that tended them and culled their fragrant produce… the fairest of these gardens were unsymmetrical ones with winding paths that led by unexpected turns to some half-hidden bower wreathed in roses… the plants of the grandmothers garden were those that had been cherished for years and years. [1]

Edgars garden and choice of flowers was deeply influenced by his family's gardens when he was a child, especially his rose arbor and

pagoda. (see chapter 5)

EDGAR'S BIRTHPLACE SUMMER, 1897

When Edgar was older, he took refuge in the woods with the flowers in his secret garden. He had few friends because he lived so far from town. In school, he was teased and bullied and often made to sit on the dunce stool which made the teasing worse.

EDGAR AT BEVERLY SCHOOL, November 25, 1890

...Later, when I was from nine to my early teens, I enjoyed a little glade in the woods, and the trees. I had my favorite little flower glen, with hazelnut bushes, pawpaws thicket, and the like.

(464-12) R27 12-1-32

...In this little bower, there was never any intrusion from those outside. It was here that I read the first letter from a girlfriend. It was here that I went to pray when my grandmother died, whom I loved so dearly and who had meant so much to me.

(464-12) R30 1-31-33

When he was sixteen, he fell in love with Bess and took her to his secret place in the woods.

The place and the girl were so sacred to me that I couldn't help tell her of some of the things that had happened there; how the place came to be made, how the little folks had dug a spring here that was, after several years, still running clear and beautiful; the flowers they had planted and that were now blooming and seemed yet to be cared for by a loving hand; how I had come here to read the first note Bess had written me in school, and had sat here to reply to her.

But all my words seemed to fall on deaf ears, for Bess laughed at me and my mysterious tale of the little people. She said she liked me but didn't care for all these things that I talked about, which to her were unnatural.[2]

Edgar said he would "...be something – maybe the best preacher in the country...[have] a lovely garden and fields of pretty crops and the like,"[3] and asked her to be his wife. But she just laughed at him and told him he was crazy to talk about such things. His heart was broken, and for a short time he was afraid he was crazy because he saw fairies, elves and "little people".

Around 1900 when he was 23, Edgar and some friends went on a picnic at Pilot Rock, an historic place in Christian County, Kentucky. Edgar climbed up on a rock ledge and was caught off-guard by the camera looking very much like an elf while communicating with nature.

He had a deep connection with all trees, and learned at a young age to talk with them.

A few years afterwards (when I had grown to be six or seven years old) our home was in a little wood. Here I learned to talk with the trees, or it appeared that they talked with me. I even yet hold that anyone may hear voices, apparently coming from a tree, if willing to choose a tree (a living tree, not a dead one) and sit against it for fifteen to twenty minutes each day (the same time each day) for twenty days. This was my experience. I chose a very lovely tree, and around it I played with my playmates that came (who then seemed very much smaller than I). We built a beautiful bower of hazelnut branches, redwood, dogwood and the like, with wild violets, Jack-in-the-Pulpit, and many of the wild mosses that seemed to be especially drawn to this particular little place where I met my friends to talk with - the little elves of the trees. How often this came, I don't know. We lived there for several years. It was there that I read the Bible through the first time, that I learned to pray, that I had many visions or experiences; not only of visioning the elves but what seemed to me to be the hosts that must have appeared to the people of old, as recorded in Genesis particularly.

...To describe these elves of the trees, the fairies of the woods, or – to me – the angels or hosts, with all their beautiful and glorious surroundings, would be almost a sacrilege. They have meant, and do yet, so very much to me that they are as rather the sacred experiences that we do not speak of – any more than we would of our first kiss, and the like. Why do I draw such comparisons? There are, no doubt, physical manifestations that are a counterpart or an expression of all the unseen forces about us, yet we have closed our eyes and our ears to the songs of the spheres, so that we are unable again to hear the voices or to see the forms take shape and minster – yea strengthen us – day by day!

(464-12) R30 1-31-33

He felt anyone could talk to the trees if they were willing to take the time and be persistent.

Personaly-have never found anything better than going out to commune with nature, sit beside a tree and meditate-and as have oft told many,dare any one to try and talk with a tree-some special tree-for several days and not get an answer back, or take the 14th of John,and put self in the place as to whom the Master is talking with, and not meet any problem of the mind.
believe you will find either or both of these worth trying some time-they will bring unbelievable things to you.

(2584) CF 8-1-40

EDGAR AND A TREE
Hopkinsville, Kentucky, [1898]

Edgar often gave lectures at the Cayce Hospital that were published in the weekly newspaper, The Virginia Beach News.

> I prayed very earnestly that afternoon as I sat in the woods by my favorite tree that had so often seemed to speak to me, answering many of my childish questions, as the birds and little animals of the section would gather about me. Even, in time, I seemed to hear the answer that God was just as near and personal as we would allow Him to be, speaking to us through his creatures.[4]

Hugh Lynn, his eldest son, had a different connection with trees and was able to move from his body into a tree without talking to it.

> I was just a part of it and caught up and just dispersed in its energy pattern. It's a very disturbing kind of feeling because you are scattered, blended like you are getting beat up in a milkshake.
> …There is an energy pattern there and when you tune yourself to that energy, you get involved in it, you know it is alive, you feel it, you hear it, you are a part of it, you are in it, so to speak, you move with the sap and you feel what is going on with the roots and leaves. The tree is a living entity, it has life and it is going places, and it perpetuates itself through its seeds and all its connections with its brothers of the same kind in the forest, but it is also part of a bigger pattern of all trees, part of an energy network.[5]

Eckhart Tolle says:

> When you look at a tree and perceive its stillness, you become still yourself. You connect with it at a very deep level. You feel a oneness with whatever you perceive in and through stillness. Feeling the oneness of yourself with all things is true love.[6]

Cyril Scott could also see the elves, fairies and gnomes as a child, and was very misunderstood - just like Edgar. He kept a diary which was published in 1953 as The Boy Who Saw True.

> There is a lovely old tree in uncle John's garden, and to-day I sat a long time watching a funny old gnome who lives inside it, like one of the gnomes in my fairy-tale book. He has great long thin legs and wears a red cap, though the rest of him is like the colour of the trunk of the tree. Sometimes he comes out of his tree and goes prancing about in the grass and looking so funny that I want to giggle, but was afraid I

might make him offended.[7]

NATURE SPIRITS

Flower Newhouse, who is highly respected for her work with the angels and nature spirits, saw them all her life. She described an Angelic Hierarchy that keeps the earth green, productive and beautiful. The lowest levels eventually work their way up to become angels.

EARTH REALM [8]

God		
Archangels		
Angels		
Devas		
Gnomes/Brownies	larger than elves	
Elves	15-24 inches high	live 300 years
Fairies	8-12 inches high	live 100 years
Elementals	1-12 inches high	

ELEMENTALS

The elementals are a teeming population that live in the etheric world and are prompted and directed by the devas. They expect us to be unselfish and generous, and it upsets them when we are not.

FAIRIES

Newhouse says the fairies "impress, quicken and energize the flowers and plants in their care through regular, rhythmic breathing that recharges the earth's surface to a depth of three feet."[9] Ted Andrews feels that anyone can connect with the Faerie *(British spelling)* Realm by taking the time to be in nature near waterways such as beaches, the seashore, rivers, ponds, wells and where streams divide. They can be found in any opening in the land, on islands, road intersections, wild areas, glades in the woods, or in our home.[10] The best times are dawn, noon, dusk, midnight, the Equinoxes and Solstices – especially June 18-21st – when contact is easiest.[11] Fairies are drawn to prayer, singing, laughter and children playing, and love classical music such as Tchaikovsky's Swan Lake or Sleeping Beauty.[12] Doreen Virtue says fairies are nature angels whose job is to protect the environment and animals. They have egos and judge us when we mistreat them, but will be kind and helpful when we are loving and kind. They want and need our help by picking up litter, especially plastic.[13]

GARDEN FAIRIES
by Pat Barnette

The fairies came to my garden today.
Oh I so wish they had come to stay.

With mornings first hint they came into view.
As from where they came, I haven't a clue.

They had hair of light beams and gauzy wings.
They were just the loveliest little things.

They all danced and whirled and twittered and flew.
Their clothing was pink and yellow and blue.

They sang and they trilled and chattered with glee.
My! They were a wonderful sight to see!

They climbed the grape arbor. What a surprise!
I could hardly believe my very own eyes!

They swung on the bluebells and Queen Anne's lace.
How I wish you could have seen my face!

They played hide and seek and peek-a-boo.
Do you think they sent to your house too?[14]

(5359) was told to draw the fairies and gnomes that she saw and make them into cards. She was very psychic, and the influence of flowers and beauty came from two incarnations with Edgar: Persia, where she loved nature – "flowers, roses, clouds, trees, water and sounds", and Egypt where she learned the art of putting colored flowers on linen. This technique was developed to aid healing in the temples and homes. In her present lifetime she was counseled not to be timid about her connection with nature.

…Don't be afraid to acknowledge that ye see fairies as ye study, for you will nurture these experiences. Don't be afraid to say that you see the gnomes which would hinder people at times. These may be a part of the background for many of the cards, for many of the various sketches which you would make.

(5359-1) T

The parents of an extremely psychic four year old boy were told it was their responsibility to train him in spiritual truths, not tell him he was unusual, or question what he saw or said. He could be the perfect channel for healing others through touch, and would bring blessings to everyone only if they heeded the guidance on how he should be raised. In a previous life in Scotland, he had also seen the Fairy Kingdom.

> …The entity began its activity as a prodigy, as one already versed in its associations with the unseen – or the elemental forces; the fairies and those of every form that do not give expression in a material way and are only seen by those who are attuned to the infinite.

(2547-1) T

(2072) asked Edgar to help her with the colors of three fairies in her aura chart that represented love, hope and faith. She wondered if the love fairy should be rose colored, and he replied:

> Should think in coloring the faeries – one would be more golden – the other more silver – and the other more blue with lots of color of course in each, but those colors predominating for each – don't you think so – what faeries have see are like that, tho do not know them by name or do I know which would be which even if you used this idea.

(2072-6) R12 3-19-42

Frances Kerr Cook, a well known book illustrator, had four readings from December 1943 to June 1944. Edgar had known her in a previous lifetime in Fort Dearborn, Michigan, and had ordered Sunday School supplies from her husband, David C. Cook Publishers, in this lifetime. Her fairy illustrations are well-known, especially Red Fairies to the Moon.

ELVES, GNOMES, BROWNIES
Newhouse says elves rank higher than fairies and are more vigorous and defined in form. They care for larger shrubs and plants over twelve feet. Gnomes – sometimes called Brownies – are more evolved larger than elves. She saw them attired in leaves and flowers, not human clothing. They have names, feel emotions like humans, and live in the rocks above and below the earth's crust.[15]
In 1942 Edgar wrote Mrs. (2441) about gnomes:

Yes,been quite interested in what many have said about the Gremlins, recall the first Gnome ever saw,and the effect it had on a gentleman visiting here.they like all unseen little folk are most interesting am sure but there seem to be good ones and bad ones-from some of the reports.would like to talk with some one who had had the experience of having them ride with them.

(2441) CF 11-24-42

In 2008, an A.R.E. staff member recalled that both she and Hugh Lynn had seen photographs of leprechauns (a fairy who can reveal hidden treasure) in the camellia bush by the ramp on the south side of the hospital building. They could not be seen with the naked eye, but if a picture was taken when there was no wind and the leaves rustled and drooped, images of two inch high, very happy leprechauns sitting on the leaves would show up on film. They had cherubic faces and wore fancy hats and suits with either dark green or plaid jackets and green bow ties.

CAMELLIA BUSH March 2009
Alas, No Leprechauns

DEVAS

According to Newhouse, Devas or shining ones, stand on the threshold of angelhood. Tree devas are very radiant and vibrant and are often mistaken for angels who supervise them. They are gifted with intelligence and sensitivity, and create much of nature's beauty, harmony and well-being of trees. She describes them as being light green with narrow, elongated faces and flashing eyes. They prefer rural and wild areas, but a few have adapted to the noise and pollution of cities.[16] We learn from the devas and they learn from us. They have a capacity for love and tenderness, and have a deep concern for others. The higher devas, who are guardians of groups of humans or nations, act as messengers to carry out the will of higher angels, archangels and the Creator. Newhouse says that the evergreens, redwoods and sequoias are the most advanced and attract the most advanced devas.[17]

Rudolph Steiner says everything is created by the Nature Spirits, including humans. "All that surrounds us - not only mineral, vegetable and animal, but we ourselves, including our bodies and inner organs – is created and maintained by nature spirits.[18] Edgar understood this for his connection with the fairies and elves was so deep that he felt something die in him when his nature sanctuary was taken away. In reading (1265), Cayce also explained that brownies, pixies, fairies and gnomes are like people.

> (Q) What is meant by the term "brownies" in the last answer of the Check Reading?
> (A) The manner in which those of the elementals - entities who have not entered into materiality - have manifested and do at times manifest themselves before or to the entity, [1265].
> Brownies, pixies, fairies, gnomes are not elementals, but elements that are as definite ENTITIES as man materialized, see?
>
> (1265-3) T

ENDNOTES

1-Adams, Restoring American Gardens p. 159
2-Smith, Robert A. *About My Father's Business* p. 24-5
3-Ibid p. 25
4-Ibid p. 171
5-Ibid p. 252-4
6-Tolle, Eckhart *Stillness Speaks* p. 5
7-Scott, Cyril *The Boy Who Saw True* p. 498
8-Newhouse, ch. 3
8-Ibid p. 36
10-Andrews, Ted *Enchantment of the Faerie Realm* p. 16-17
11-Ibid p. 14
12-Ibid p. 208-9
13-Virtue, Doreen *Fairies 101* p. 2, 5
14-Garden Fairies poem by Pat Barnette, A.R.E. member, June 23, 1990
15-Newhouse p. 37-8
16-Ibid p. 40-1
17-Ibid p. 23
18-Tompkins p. 112

Mrs. (464)'s "Toy Garden"

Chapter Four
Mrs. (464)

The Indians, you know, were hard to fool. Their closeness to nature
enabled them to obtain through their intuitive forces much
that we would do well to learn.   (2457) CF 3-30-32

A 51 year old woman (464) who had been a semi-invalid for thirteen
years, had her first reading for multiple health problems on June 22, 1926.
She wrote Edgar 2-3 times a week and complained constantly. She had
trouble understanding the suggestions and felt it was a waste of time and
money. Edgar had his hands full as he counseled her with the patience of
a saint through her forty-seven readings over a period of nineteen years.
In December, 1926, he wrote a close friend:

> Yes, just as I have said, she, Mrs. [464], has every ailment that she
> has ever heard anyone has, and partically every symptom that anyone
> may describe to her become her own symptoms. Now, I don't mean to
> infer xx by this that she is nutty unbalanced, or anything of the kind,
> but one of those nerve inclined people, who either pitch everything on
> the other fellow or take every symptom to themselves.
>
> (2457) CF 12-17-26

Eleven months after her first reading, he bluntly told her:

> I'm sure you have realized already, Mrs. [464], that the information
> given isn't worth anything unless the individual will honestly attempt
> to apply same in their own life – for to go at anything half heartedly,
> is to already acknowledge defeat – but youcannot be an exception to
> the many hundreds and hundreds of people, unless you already have
> made up your mind, "Well, it ain't any use – it won't work on me,"
> for of course if you make up your mind that way, it won't!
>
> (464) CF 4-25-27

Edgar often spoke of the earth as a garden for our soul growth.[1] They had
known each other in past lives: in Fort Dearborn, Michigan when she was
an Indian and Edgar was Bainbridge, a drunkard and gambler, and in
Egypt where she sought the return of the high priest, RA-TA (Edgar),
from exile. From the very first letter, Edgar felt a close connection to both

her and her family. They had a great deal in common in this life with their love of nature, flowers and gardening. In 1931 she was (temporarily) feeling better and began to mention flowers in her letters. They became garden pen-pals, and over the years she sent him many bulbs, cuttings, seeds and flowers. In 1932, after he had moved to his last home on Arctic Crescent, she wrote about her "toy garden."

I received your lovely letter & so glad to meet in with another flower grower all of my life time I have loved a garden & have never had a real garden yet. I have planted trees only for some one else to enjoy the fruit of. the place where we live now we only have a very small space. You might call it a toy garden. I have always been obliged to live in the city & I love the country best. I will surely send you some plants we have what is called an African violet it is a house plant: some call it a begonia it is like a violet I am goingnto send you some leaves of it as it grows freely from a leaf, put the leaves in water & let them stay there until they root and make a little plant then pot them. we have a baby plant full of bloom now. I don't just understand your violets blooming all through the winter months. You must have a very fine climate where you are. but I always thought violets bloomed only for a season of their own. our wild violets are not the least bit fragrant and not so deep a purple as the domesticated violet. the violet seeds down without flowers. no wonder they spread so fast. I should think that you could have some very fine Iris on that place where you are. I have a few but no choice varieties I love them I would like to have some bulbs for the spring but there is no use thinking about it I can't have them I like tulips & narcissis & daffidils & so on.
…I have some Ageratum a plant that spreads a lot and blooms late in the fall. it is a lavender fuzzy flower I can send you some of that it is not the least bit particular where it grows so long as it gets going all you do is plant it and say sickum it is prettier in masses. I will send it a little later on. I want to put in a dahlia bulb or two they are only common varieties but are so pretty one a pure white tinged with pink that I like so well indeed some of their finer brothers and sisters are too big and clumsy to suit me. a flower too big to hold its head up is not so nice. allthough there are some very handsome dahlias now we have several Dahlia growers in and around Cleveland who raise exhibition flowers & it is a joy to visit their gardens. however as usual I must be content with a commoner variety. I am afraid you will be tired of reading this rambling letter. I never could say anything in 3 words.

I am always interested in your work. & I wish I could meet you personaly.

(464) CF 11-10-32

Edgar replied six days later and spoke of the power of God in the flowers that gave her a more spiritual understanding of gardening.

...I want you to know how very much I appreciate your taking the time to write me as you have, and for your being so thoughtful and considerate as to send me such a lovely box of bulbs, flowers and the like. You know from your own self, I am sure, what a tender spot you touched when you get into that field which is to me, possibly, just a hobby; but I love growing things. As we look into the face of a rose, a violet, or any of the rest of creation, we can and do know that the very life of it, which no man has ever been able to even find or produce, is a manifestation in the material world of that force and power we call God. That it has taken and does take all kinds of forms is very wonderful to us, but it should make us realize the fact in our mental consciousness that His love, beauty and power is so all-encompassing as to include everything. Whatever it is that enables the African violet to gather the necessary elements from the earth, air and the environ in which man puts it, to make the most beautiful blossom it can from that with which it has to work, gives pleasure to us who love to see them. Whatever it is that enables the dahlia, be it the commonest variety or that man has cultivated, to give that beauty and strength, that enables it to draw such rich color from its environs, the impelling force, I SAY, is from that very Source we worship as God. That he is mindful of these things that will add to the joy and pleasure of our poor mortal lives is a lesson, a sermon in itself. If we will but trust Him as they do we will fulfill that purpose for which we came into the earth, just as they do; while possibly not in the richness that some are able to attain under other environs or that have responded differently to those conditions about them, yet with all the strength of that given us if we will use our own surroundings the very best we can, as does the little violet, the dahlia or any of these, then we realize we are fulfilling that He would have us do. They grumble not, as we know of, when we fail to supply them water, or if we allow the insects to come in and destroy; yet they do the best they can with what they have to do with.

(464-12) R25 11-16-32

She in turn spoke about honeysuckle in the South. Edgar also loved the old-fashioned coral and sweet varieties which always had a place in his garden.

Dear Mr. Cayce,...
...While in the South the fragrance of the wild honeysuckle could be smelt as we drove along the roads. I cannot put into words my thoughts & feelings. the moonlight night the balmy spring air the fragrance of the honeysuckle was intoxicating   I was lifted out of myself I belonged to another world.

(464) CF 11-26-32

They both had problems growing peach trees: hers became infested with worms and the only peach tree that bore fruit for Edgar had to be moved to make room for an addition to store the readings.

Dear Mr. Cayce,...
...It has always seemed to me that apples, pears and peach trees are a man's job. I had one peach tree here in my garden it grew from a stone that someone carelessly threw away & because it was a baby peach tree I allowed it to grow not paying much attention to it until it reached proportions that I tho't needed pruning back a bit so it wouldn't shade too much of my garden. so I cut it back to 3 stems like this ψ saying that will hold you. next year in the fall I gave that tree a sizing up with one eye closed and the other squinting for each one of those three prongs gave forth 3 more prongs. a yard and a half long. making 9 prongs. & I wondered is that the way of all peach trees? so I studied for a while. what to do with it so I cut it back again. next year it had a few blossoms. on and 3 peaches developed. and a lot more of wood. the peaches were large good flavor & good colour yellow. only did not ripen until nearly snow time so late so the next year there was a lot of peaches. but the tree had grown so that it covered too much space both in our yard and the neighbors. the next year it was a full grown overgrown tree full of wormy peaches that we could not use we had no way of spraying it so I looked it over went in the house got the saw and sawed off all the limbs and Martin helped me dig it up. & that was the end of the peach tree like Jack and the beanstalk.

(464) CF 1-22-33

As she shared her love for gardening and nature, her letters helped him immensely during a very difficult time when he was recovering from the loss of his garden and the hospital. When she asked asked about his childhood and playmates, she touched on something very special.

My oldest daughter, [2144], asked me to write you on a subject that I think you know something about. Sometime ago in one of your letters to me you wrote that people used to call you a strange child, that you had playmates that no one could see but yourself.

…Now if you are interested and have time to write, I would be very pleased if you would tell me of some of your childhood days' experiences with your invisible playmates.

(464-12) R29 1-27-33

It was a subject he rarely spoke about and he immediately answered at length.

…The questions you ask are very interesting and, to me, very much worth while. All through the years I think I have been (possibly from necessity quite a matter of fact individual. No doubt all my childhood and boyhood associates were also quite a matter of fact.) Consequently, I have gotten far away from many of the experiences that were very near and dear to me as a little child. As I look back upon the various experiences I rather persuade myself they have been steps in my development. Perhaps if I had paid more attention to them the present would be quite different.

I don't know whether or not I can give you sufficient insight to be worth while, as to just what took place during those experiences of my early childhood when I visited unseen playmates; for I will have to admit that – except for a general outline of my life, in which this subject is touched on just a little – I have never attempted to put those experiences in writing. So, if my letter appears somewhat disconnected or unreasonable, know that it is because of a physically developed body (and possibly a sane mind) attempting to keep within the bounds of reason.

Except the fairy stories of Grimm and Hans Andersen, I have never read of others' experiences. While I have had a little correspondence with Sir Arthur Conan Doyle, and have one or two of his books, I have not read the one you mention. I would love very much to read it, and will see if my son can obtain it from the Norfolk library.

These are at least some of my experiences. As to just what was the first experience, I don't know. The one that appears at present to be among the first, was when I was possibly eighteen or twenty months old. I had a playhouse in the back of an old garden, among the honeysuckle and other flowers. At that particular time much of this garden had grown up in tall reeds, as I remember. I had made a little shelter of the tops of the reeds, and had been assisted by an unseen playmate in weaving or fastening them together so they so they would form a shelter. On pretty days I played there. One afternoon my mother came down the garden walk calling me. My playmate (who appeared to me to be about the same size as myself) was with me. It had never occurred to me that he was not real, or that he wasn't one of the neighbors' children, until my mother spoke and asked me my playmate's name. I turned to ask him but he disappeared. For a time this disturbed my mother somewhat, and she questioned me at length. I remember crying because she had spied upon me several times, and each time the playmate would disappear.

About a year or eighteen months later, this was changed considerably – as to the number of playmates. We had moved to another country home. Here I had two favorite places where I played with these unseen people. One (very peculiarly) was in an old graveyard where the cedar trees had grown up. Under a cedar tree, whose limbs had grown very close to the ground, I made another little retreat, where – with these playmates – I gathered bits of colored glass, beautifully colored leaves and things of that nature from time to time. But, what disturbed me was that I didn't know where they came from nor why they left when some of my family approached. The other retreat was a favorite old strawstack that I used to slide down. This was on the opposite side of the road (main highway) from where we lived, and in front of the house. The most outstanding experience (and one that I am sure disturbed her much) was when my mother looked out a window and saw children sliding down this strawstack with me. Of course, I had a lovely little retreat dug out under the side of the straw ring, in which we often sat and discussed the mighty problems of a three or four year old child. As my mother looked out, she called to ask who were the children playing with me. I realized I didn't know their names. How were they dressed, you ask? There were boys and girls. It would be impossible (at this date) to describe their dress, figure or face, yet it didn't then – nor does it now - occur to me that they were any different from myself, except that they had the ability to appear or disappear as our moods changed. Just once I looked out the window from the house and saw the fairies [little folk] there, beckoning me to come and play. That time also my mother saw them very plainly, but she didn't make any objection to my going out to play with them. This experience, as I remember now, lasted during a whole season – or summer.

…Possibly there are many questions you would ask, as to what games we played. Those I played with at the haystack were different from those in the graveyard, or in the garden. Those I played with in the wood were different. They seemed to fit more often to what would interest or develop me. To say they planted the flowers or selected the bower, or the little cove in which my retreat was built, I don't think would be stretching it at all, or that they tended these or showed me – or talked to me of – their beauty. It was here that I first learned to read. Possibly the hosts on high gave me my first interpretation of that we call the Good Book. I do not think I am stretching my imagination when I say such a thing. We played the games of children, we played being sweethearts, we played being man and wife, we played being sisters and brothers, we played being visitors and preachers. We played being policemen and the culprits. We played being all the things that we knew about us.

No, I never have any of these visions now, or – if any – very rarely.

In a reading one time, it was said by those present that I waxed very eloquent in regard to these very experiences, when we were attempting to locate some minerals or oil on the land where I lived as a child (for all these places where I lived were only a mile or so apart). Two stenographers were attempting to write this reading, but failed to get any of it; so what I am telling you is thirdhand information. Those present reported that they were awestruck, as if they were in the presence of something that prevented them from even moving – except to smile or weap for joy. It seems that as soon as I became unconscious, according to their reports, a conversation started between many others and myself – but only my voice could be heard. Many questions were asked by the one conducting the reading at the time, but there would only be the reiteration of those days we had spent together – and of their longing for me to soon join them, that we might continue with all the things we had enjoyed during those days. This conversation, they said, continued for almost three hours, and the seven individuals present were even afraid to approach me when I was finally awakened. The one with whom I had been very close was afraid to even sleep in the same room with me that night.

But, as all such experiences, it was gradually explained away by our beautiful material-mindedness – saying it was nothing but imagination and the like.

What it all means, I don't know that I can comprehend or understand. As I have said to you before, all manifestations must be of that divine influence or force we call God. All forms of life, seen and unseen, are essences and manifestations of that One.

...Now, I hope all this reminiscing will at least be worth while. It is only my experience. I'm not asking anyone to believe it. We can't experience for another. We may only see the effects of what another has visioned or experienced, in the manner of life lived by another – and then judge by that which the individual has set as the standard.

(464-12) R30 1-31-33

She loved his reply, and Edgar wrote back:

I'm glad you enjoyed my experience as to the little folks during the early portion of my life. To me these experiences are quite sacred, and I rarely speak of them.

We are having quite a blizzard here; although the sun is shining brightly this morning. The thermometer last night dropped from sixty to about twenty-two this morning, but the sun makes it look warm and beautiful outside.

(464) CF 2-9-33

Dear Mr. Cayce,...

...I don't blame you for not telling about the Fairies who would believe our report? I loved that book of Arthur Conon Doyle's about the Fairies. I was sitting on the porch one still day and I saw a leaf on the woodbine twirling around. out of an ordinary movement. & I wondered at it. what ails that leaf. It was twirling around at a great rate. I couldn't see anything but now I know what did it.

(464) CF 2-15-33

Dear Mrs. [464]:-...

I appreciate what you say about my experience during childhood. Such things are rather sacred, and we are not always made to feel very good by repeating them to people who have little or no vision.

(464-13) R5 2-21-33

The " little people" or " little folk" were not fairies. They were invisible playmates who had first and last names, parents, brothers and sisters, and prepared Edgar for future events in his life. They later incarnated and Edgar recognized them when they came for a reading. All of them became very involved in Edgar's work and the A.R.E. His grandparents supported his belief and his mother could also see them. When he shared his experiences with an aunt, she thought he had the devil in him and should be seen by a doctor. Fortunately, she was ignored, and he learned not to talk about them to anyone. December 1931, ten months after the hospital closed, he had an interesting dream.

> …I was a little boy again. Saw the fairies or elves I used to play with, and among them I recognized [[341], [849], [419] and [295]]. I seemed to reason with myself that they were just as real when I was a little boy, and they were still in the spirit world, as they are now in physical life.
>
> (294-128) T

In 1938, Edgar had a vision about his playmates and wrote about it in his diary. They were all incarnated when he had these two experiences.

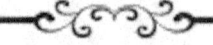

Mar.25th 1938 Diary

don't wonder,one is at times thought curious,unreasonable yes,plain nutty when they relate some of their experiences,that to them are very real.like last evening,know I was not a sleep, and dont think it was purely imagination,but- years ago as a child used to see talk with play with,those that some told me did not exist,these came to me in one two and a few times as many as three at once,and were not always the same,some times boys and some times girls, they told me their names,when they were with me and we played together.but last evening they all came at once,eight of them, five boys and three girls-their first question was do you remember us and to be sure I did,no they appear not to have grown any,why,did they want to play,no,then what-when will you be with us again to discuss the things we used to?
what does it mean ,I do not know,am just wondering will they come again.

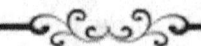

Mrs. (464) had a way of talking about nature and her garden that gave Edgar much joy, and another letter in March was all about summer flowers.

Dear Mr. Cayce,...
...In August our fields are covered with the purple aster, the golden rod and michelmas daisy. purple iron weed and some boneset It surely is a gorgeous sight. In July, we have our fields covered with white dog daisies or margerites. occasionally we find a patch of black eyed Susan daisies the wild gardens are beautiful. florists are cultivating the wild aster now but why? it grows in abundance everywhere. did you ever see a lawn carpeted with dandelions in full bloom. they rival the sunshine. A friend of mine & I slipped into a bit of wild wood one day we were as guilty as guilty could be we felt that we were trespassing & no doubt we were. but luck was with us we were not seen. it was one of the loveliest wild flower gardens I was ever in. white and red trilliums squirrel corn & dutch mans breeches. Wild ginger & many other varieties. as Violets wild forget-me not ferns.
& plants of delicate green foliage fern like: that was a treat that day we often speak of it and laugh. I have never come across the blue gentian either open or bottle & I have never seen any lady slippers in all of my wanderings through the woods. I believe I like the spring wild flowers better than summer and fall flowers.
...Flowers are my hobby and when I get started on them I am carried away with the subject.

(464) CF 3-10-33

Six weeks later Edgar was helping Hugh Lynn build a boy scout cabin and inhaling springtime.

Dear Mrs. [464]:-
Just a line to let you hear from us again. We are having quite a beautiful spell at the present time, following a few days of bad and stormy weather. The woods and the country around here are very beautiful; the woods especially. Our oldest boy, who is Assistant Scoutmaster for the Boy Scouts here, is erecting a cabin on a plot in the woods, adjoining the bay where the famous Lynnhaven Oysters are obtained. A few times I have been out with him. I have two boys, you know – the older one twenty-six, and the other fifteen. The dogwood is in bloom, the wild honeysuckle, and an innumberable number of plants; wild violets, bluebells, redbuds; and many, many,

that I know little or nothing about.   They are very, very pretty.

(464) CF 4-26-33

In 1934, they discussed nicotine which Edgar had never heard of.

Dear Mr. Cayce,…
…I planted Nicotine one year & I have had them ever since I planted
petunias & I have had them ever since too I planted portulaca & I have
had that too. they are like a weed pest. nicotine has tomato worms on
them did you ever see any of those fellows? Ugh! I just give them a
little drink of Paris green. where is the potatoe bug when there is no
potatoes. tell me will you? just as soon as the potatoe vines appear
there are the bugs too ..I am a city farmer I cannot answer that
question. I try to plant flowers that make a nice bouquet for the table.

(464) CF 1-22-34

Dear Mrs. [464]:-…
I haven't seen many of the plants you refer to.   I'm not familiar with
the nicotine plant, though in looking it up in the catalog I find that it's
supposed to be some kind of flowering tobacco.   Well, I've seen
plenty of tobacco of all kinds, but I can't imagine anyone having a very
pleasant odor from a tobacco plant.   This must be, then, something
entirely different.   I'll try to get hold of some of it if I can.

(464) CF 2-17-34

Dear Mr. Cayce,…
…I am sending you some Nicotine seed they are a night blooming
flower & delightfully fragrant in my garden they become a weed. and
flourish in the sand. I pull them up by the roots. petunias do the same
thing they do not come true to colour they self sew and come up
different shades. this summer I want to plant some phlox seed, the
annual. they are gay little flowers. and they don't grow too high
…I love to tramp through the woods in the spring time I musn't
complain now for I have enjoyed that pleasure. off & on ever since I
was a child. but flowers seem to be getting scarcer all the time. or else
we go to the wrong place for them.

(464) CF 2-27-34

Dear Mr. Cayce,…
 May be you will be sorry when you get that nicotine started. It like
 some people that you can't get rid of.

(464) CF 5-14-34

They shared the ups and downs of their gardens and both made jam and canned vegetables such as tomatoes, okra and beans. This was Edgar's favorite part of gardening; however, the very thought of it made her want to lie down and rest. Her health was a constant roller coaster of ups and downs, and she was always pessimistic and upset because of her physical limitations. In 1936, she wrote that too many flowers had self-seeded and ants disturbed some roots which killed the plants. Edgar wasn't having much luck either and had to keep replanting because of dry weather, but he never complained or felt it was a hardship.

Dear Mrs. [464]:-...
Have been at work in my little garden,have had a little rain so it looks some better,is mighty higeldapilgerty – or something like that. for there have been so many replantings from the dry weather,nothing came up very well but possibly that will make the season for each plant last that much longer, some of the flowers didn't show up,so dug them up and planted others now all have come up,so you can see how they would look
(464) CF 6-19-36

Dear Mrs. [464)]:-...
...Garden has done well this year. have plenty of mellons just now but they do no last very long two or three weeks is about all I think,but very nice to run out in the garden and get the mellons for breakfast.
(464) CF 8-19-36

She was at *her* best when she wrote about nature, such as the fall colors in Canada where she grew up.

...We are having most delightful weather the past few days. but not growing weather everything has ripened down now & the leaves are falling fast but I have never seen anything here to equal the beauty of the big sugar maples in Canada around our old home they turn every colour from pale yellow to darkest reds,. rose shades & dull lavenders . in every shade of each colour a glorious sight many a thrill I have had gazing up at a tree that was like a shower of gold. to me they are beautiful beyond description for there is a feeling that goes with it one of gladness and of sadness. a longing to hold to preserve such beauty. only to see it gently seemingly laughingly spirited away in the silently falling leaves. until what was a glorious sight yesterday is only a memory today such is life.

(464) CF 9-28-38

And Edgar was at *his* best when he reminded her of nature and God during her difficult times.

> **...sorry tho you are feeling so badly,but there is hope am sure,for so long as you can appreciate the beauty of nature,all hope hasnt gone,its when one gets to the point tey dislike such as the lovely weather-the Blue sky-and the like and feel they are just tormenting them is the condition hopeless.For God is still at HOME and –it isnt the boys at all that run things.**

(464) CF 9-27-39

Visits to Cleveland and the beach were planned frequently, but they only met once when she came to see him in June, 1937. He wanted her to receive hands-on-healing because her case was so difficult. During World War II when their correspondence dwindled because he was so overwhelmed by thousands of requests for readings, he wrote a sad but humorous letter.

> I certainly owe you an apology for not writing to you sooner, but we can always find excuses and mine is that I have been sick; I have been away; I have been mean; I have been dirty; I have been ugly, and all sorts of things is the reason I didn't write.
> …You know when I have been sick how swamped I get with mail. Not only have we had to disappoint dozens of people, but have sorta made them mad because we haven't been able to do something about it.

(464) CF 3-7-44

In the end, the last thing they had in common was the loss of a garden: she was too ill and Edgar was too busy.

ENDNOTES

1-Talk by Harmon Bro at Pilgrim Institute 1988. Bro was a minister, psychotherapist, teacher, writer, and inspirational lecturer who lived with Edgar and worked closely with him before he died.

ROSE ARBOR
A birds eye view
June 1931

Chapter Five

SECOND GARDEN - 115 WEST 35th STREET
September 1925 – May 1931

Learn also from the flower that where thou art, ye, too, may make that place more beautiful for your being there, whether it is in this or that or whatever place. Whether in the hovel or in the home of the mighty, make it beautiful as do the flowers.   (5122-1) T

On September13, 1925, Edgar moved to Virginia Beach from Dayton, Ohio. Three days later he settled into a summer house (now 315 Arctic Ave) that just had a fireplace for heat.[1] "…it was the only cottage within three blocks of Pacific and Atlantic Avenues. The forlorn two-story white-frame cottage…sat among a grid of empty lots on a weed-choked square situated halfway between the sea to the east and pine barrens to the west. There was no driveway, no garage, not even a walkway to the cement steps leading up to the open porch and front door."[2]

115 West 35th Street
late September 1925

115 West 35th Street Back View
late September 1925

It had been rented sight unseen, then purchased for them the following year by Morton Blumenthal. He and his brother Edwin, had met Cayce and offered to finance a 30 bed Hospital for Research and Enlightenment at 105th Street and Atlantic Avenue (now 67th Street). As Thomas Sugrue said, "It was a long, hard road for Edgar Cayce, from the first fairy voice of childhood to the first ground broken for the Cayce Hospital."[3] After he had to leave his secret retreat in the woods in 1891, Edgar had not been able to have a garden for 34 years because of frequent moves from one rental to another and a precarious financial situation.

> …It was a great trouble to me when we moved away from that little home and I had to leave all the trees, vines and flowers that had come to mean so much to me. From then on, [1891] until I moved to Virginia Beach some seven years ago, [1925] I had little opportunity to enjoy a flower garden. Something seemed to have been killed.
>
> (464-12) R27 12-1-32

But now that dead part could come alive again with a secure home and income. He was able to have his first garden and re-kindle the connection with nature and the fairies. It was a very small lot and he managed to plant every square inch. He started a rose arbor with cuttings his sister Mary sent him, built a garage and trellis in the backyard and made two flower boxes for the front windows.

115 West 35th Street
Summer 1926

Garage and Trellis in Backyard
Summer 1926

A year after moving in, he wrote his mother who was too sick to visit:

> …I know you would like, though, to see the place around here. I have
> a few chickens now, and a little gardening space, so I putter around
> with them once in a while. We have some mighty nice turnip greens
> and turnips coming on – mustard and spinach. Of course our
> chickens are all young ones and haven't gotten big enough to
> commence laying yet. I'm in hopes we'll have some eggs this Fall and
> winter – have a very nice place for the chickens, though not a very
> large run. I hope they'll do good.
>
> (3776) CF 9-30-26

Mrs. (2457) sent more chickens and two of the baby roosters adored him.

> The chickie biddies, as I wrote you, arrived alright. Everyone as
> spy [spry] and pert as you please, and I think some of them must have
> at some time or another been somebody's particular pets, for they
> insist on meeting me at the gate, and will step up on my hand or
> shoulder any time. But I think these are little roosters – these two
> special pets! None of these, I don't believe, have begun to lay yet,
> but the change and the cold weather I amsure has had a heap to do
> with it, and I hope they will though real soon. I certainly do thank
> you – certainly appreciate your kindness – and I'm sure they will be a
> joy and pleasure to me personally anyway, very, very often - for it
> gives me something to putter around with, and of course I remember
> you helped me to build the henhouse, and now the hens are in it why
> it makes it all different. One of the others I had has begun to lay
> every day or two. I think I'll have enough eggs of my own hen's
> laying to make a cake for Christmas –
>
> (2457) CF 12-17-26

He always felt close to God with tools in his hands, and was out digging
in his garden in January.

> I'm mighty glad to say I'm feeling a lot better than I have been for a
> good long while, physically. The weather has turned off warm and
> real pretty, and of course I commenced piddling around and digging
> around outside. I don't know what I'd have the back yard looking
> like if they'd give me enough time. I hope it won't look too much like
> a mare's nest. The chickens are doing pretty well, though several of
> them look like they've got the 'pip' or something worse; I don't know
> what. I guess it'll be the survival of the fittest – perhaps I just have too

many in such a small place – it's kind of like our flowers were last summer – some of them naturally choked the rest of them to death.

(254-34) R1 1-20-27

Chickens bring many blessings - food, eggs and fertilizer - and are a major part of a garden. Edgar let them run loose and they ate more than insects.

Well, most of our flowers we planted have come up, but the UP was principally done by the chickens I think – though I think there are considerable zinnias that are coming along alright.   Possibly the others will in time if the chickens did not get them.

(254-34) R5 5-2-27

Edgar frequently wrote his eldest son when he was away at college.

Dear Hugh Lynn:-
    Well, our flowers are not doing well at all. I have gotten most of the chickens cornered, though, except the little ones that I've had to do the mothering of. I "kinder" thought they were most too little to pen up as yet – maybe I'd better let 'em get a little better start. The oldest ones are big enough now to grease a skillet.   I'm in hopes that penning them up doesn't make them lose some of their weight, nor hinder them from growing.   Now I'll try to get another start with the flowers.   A few things, though, are coming along right nicely.
…I have a lot more little chickens, but we had our old rooster for dinner yesterday – put him up and fattened him, and he sure was good!   Not setting any hens, for I think I have about as many as I can handle, when the rest are hatched.   We already have between fifty and sixty, with forty or fifty more eggs setting.   We are not getting an over abundance of eggs, but have enough to get along without buying any.
    Our strawberries are getting ripe.   I've had enough to have on my cereal a time or two, and I think there's enough there for several more times, if they get ripe.   I put a canvas over them to keep the birds away, and now that the chickens are hemmed up maybe it'll still be better. They were eating them off pretty bad.
    The rest of the garden – what there is of it – looks pretty well.

(341) CF 5-9-27

Dear Hugh Lynn:-
    Well, I got my rose garden all prepared, and have written the rose growers to know whether it's done right or not.   I'm anxious to see

them in the ground and growing.   I guess I'll be watching them every day when I do put them in.

(341) CF 9-23-27

Dear Hugh Lynn:-
…We are having some beautiful weather; and it makes me want to work outdoors – though I think I have gotten most everything fairly well in shape, and as your mother says, I'm beginning to tear down that I may build up again.   I'm fixing me a rose garden [Gertrude's favorite flower] and planting me some trees, you know.   My rose garden is on the East side between the two places.   I was glad I had it fixed before our neighbors moved in - or were you here when I started fixing it?

(341) CF 10-5-27

Dear Hugh Lynn:-
Well, things are looking right nice around the place.   I got a right nice jolt yesterday though. While it was kind of damp I thought it the best time to clean the old vines off of the pagoda, so climbing around over it I made a mis-step, and one of the beams flew up and hit me across the "chist".   I'm rather sore to-day.   I think I'll have to rest for several days now.   But we've got a right nice border laid out in preparation for a nice bed next summer.   I hope it does well. Something to mess with anyway. Some of our chickens have been having kind of a hard time keeping on laying, as they've been losing most of their feathers.

(341) CF 10-14-27

PAGODA IN BACK YARD (built by Edgar) June 1928

Dear Hugh Lynn:-

Well, things are running on about the same about the place. I've done a little more work - got my roses all planted now – got my trees yesterday and got them planted, so I guess I'm about ready for the winter weather and to wait for the developments in the Spring.

(341) CF 11-3-27

Dear Hugh Lynn:-

Four hens setting. Garden in pretty good shape. Watermelon and cantaloupe hills made – shrubbery here to put out, but didn't have all my ground in shape, so had to put it off for a few days. Fix it though when the ground is right - hope we'll have some nice looking place next summer.

(341) CF 2-25-28

Dear Hugh Lynn:-

Strawberries and chickens will be about ripe in a week or ten days. If I could save the strawberries until you get here I would save the chickens too. Out of the first sixteen I think there were fifteen roosters. That will make us a pretty good start. Strawberries are beautiful! They won't be ripe though for another week. The rest of the things look kinder under the
weather - and most of the weather has been bad.

(341) CF 5-4-28

He sent some chickens to Gladys' mother and shared his special relationship with them.

Well, I'm glad the chickens got there alright. I was mighty glad to send them, and I just hope they give you as much pleasure as it gave me to send them, and as mine do me. I think every single one I have knows me from everybody else. So that gives you some idea of how I feel about each and everyone of them. I know that two or possibly three of those sent you were rather young. All of them, of course, were last spring and summer chickens – but one of them should be laying real soon.

(1187) CF 1-17-28

His father helped with the garden while the moles munched on his bulbs.

Beautiful weather here, and naturally Pa and I do a good deal of piddling around the place – and I think everything looks pretty nice.

79

I have about sixty little chickens – pretty nice looking garden place. We are having lettuce – soon will be having asparagus and radishes. Strawberries are in bloom and the prettiest little violet bed you nearly ever saw! The crocus and hyacinths are blooming, but might look a whole lot better – the moles won't let 'em alone.

(340) CF 3-27-28

By July, the garden had expanded onto neighboring vacant lots. He was extremely busy for ground had been broken to build the hospital.

Chickens? Goodness! We have the nicest lot you ever saw! We haven't had to buy a chicken this year, nor very many vegetables. And eggs! about all we can eat. And we've got the nicest watermelon patch you ever saw. Mr. L.B., you know, is here, and he is some gardener; in fact, I'm sure you wouldn't recognize this place as being the same. If I do say it, it is nice looking, and every foot of ground is in use, and then some – for we are farming on the other fellow's lots.

(2457) CF 7-17-28

In September, he shared a chicken experience with a sister. The interesting thing is that Edgar knew exactly who each hen was, what she did and when.

Glad to say we are all fairly well. Nothing very strange or new. I believe I have something though rather strange I'll tell you, and wouldn't Mother laugh if she could hear this! As you know, we have a few chickens. Don't think Pa has told you about this – maybe He has, but I have a hen that was hatched out the 5th of March – she started laying the 6th day of August. The 15th of September she went to setting, and just for the novelty of the thing I set her. Did you ever hear of a hen nesting the same year in which she was hatched? I never did!

(243) CF 9-22-28

In the spring of 1929, he planted roses around the hospital and was talking to his pansies.

Our violets this year have been beautiful. The roses have started off wonderfully well, but the wind and dry weather recently makes them look kind of shabby – but our honeysuckle is beautiful, and the stocks – or phlox, whichever it is – are pretty; and the pansy bed looks like it might be wanting to talk to you.   In fact, I think most of the flowers are looking pretty well.   Planted a few roses around the hospital early – today I cut four beautiful buds off of them.   Looks to me as if they were rather ambitious.   Haven't had enough rain recently though to make our grass grow as I would like for it to around the hospital; neither has it been so it could grow much here in the yard – looks kind of shabby.

(2457) CF 5-7-29

Even though the hospital and readings kept him extremely busy, he always had time for his beloved garden. It is amazing how much he had been able to grow in a small area.

Speaking of back yards, you should see this one.   It is very much of a wilderness, but rather a pretty one I think.   Since Christmas there have been blossoms of some kind.   Violets – I never saw such violets outside of a greenhouse!   Then the other flowers have come along from time to time.   Several peach trees were just beautiful, and if they never have any fruit the blossoms were certainly very much worth while.   Then the apples, pears, cherries, plums. The honeysuckle, the phlox and stocks, and the fleur de lis – or flags, all in bloom. The roses are just beginning to open.   All in all, it's certainly very pretty, to think we may have to walk out and leave it any day.   The chickens are coming along very nicely, too.   Put off the last hen this morning – have something over a hundred little chicks, with about twenty-five of the older ones – still getting plenty of eggs to supply us, and in another two weeks I think we will be ready to begin on the fried chicken.   Plenty of onions and considerable asparagus in the garden; beans, tomatoes, okra, beets, plenty of radishes – we are supplying the whole neighborhood. although they grow only in a little bed in the yard along the flower bed.

(2457) CF 5-16-31

When the hospital closed (ch. 8), he also lost his home, and on May 31, 1931 moved to 105th street and the oceanfront (now 6610 67th Street). He was able to transplant a few rose bushes and violets, pick all the flowers, grapes, berries, green apples and beans and dig up the carrots and beets, but had to leave the rest behind. Edgar photographed his spectacular roses in full bloom.

Seventeen months later he was telling Mrs. (464) about his first garden.

…I appreciate very much your telling me about your garden, and troubles with it. For so many years I had little opportunity to plant anything in the ground, or have flowers around us, that since I have been at Virginia Beach all the time the family tell me that I spend every spare nickel I can get hold of, and a lot I shouldn't, on trying to have things like that around me. In the first place I lived here [115 West 35th

St., Va. Beach] I had quite an assortment on a very small lot, for though I only had about 140 x 50 feet, including the house and garage, I had fruit trees of every description almost – pear, plum, cherry, peach, apple, grapes, as well as a little garden, though I couldn't make this very large, but I had a very nice asparagus bed, onions, beans and tomatos, as well as a little bed here and there of strawberries, raspberries, blackberries, and – of course – an old fashioned garden with roses, violets and the like.

(464-12) R23 10-21-32

Five weeks later, Edgar was again rambling down memory lane to her.

…Then I spent myself in fixing up a place here that I thought was mine. I had not only a beautiful old-fashioned garden (consisting of bleeding hearts, peonies, Jack-in-the-pulpit, Tom Thumbs, Batchelor Buttons, hardy pinks, a beautiful bed of violets, pansies, gladiolli, buttercups, marcissus, snowdrops, tulips, foxglove, etc.) but fruit trees of every variety almost; apples, peaches, pears, plums, grapes, cherries, with a wonderful row of about twenty-five varieties of roses; to say nothing of a few chickens, a vegetable garden (with a wonderful asparagus bed), etc. All this on a 50 x 150 lot. Can you imagine? No, it wasn't a mess! It was very, very nicely laid out. There wasn't a lot of any, of course, but what a joy they were to me!

(464-12) R27 12-1-32

ENDNOTES

1-The house is now in the City of Virginia Beach Historical Register, Property 27
2-Kirkpatrick p. 346
3-(1800-15) R2 12/29

EDGAR'S FLOWER by TJ Davis, [1939]

Chapter Six
FLOWERS, ROSES, AND VIOLETS

Then who may tell the rose where or when to bloom? For it takes from whatever may be its surroundings, and when encompassed even by man it does the best possible to be the beauty, the joy, and to give out that which is pleasing in the service to God. (2778-2) T

FLOWERS

Ann Ree Colton says, "The flower is a vessel of grace given to man that he might receive in his most depressed hours a confirmation of God, His beauty and His glory everywhere… Flowers are a feminine aspect of Nature. All Flora Angels work with the feminine side of their androgynous powers. Thus, flowers are a tender testimony reflecting the beauty as given of God. When one is stirred by the beauty within a flower, something of compassion, of tenderness, and of reverence enters into his being. Therefore, he comes closer to the angels when he is surrounded by flowers. His soul-capacity is enlarged and his mind ennobled when he contemplates the origin and intent of flowers and their service to man…flowers are ambassadors of healing and joy."[1]

Edgar's real passion was flowers and he pressed them and kept a flower book since he was eighteen. "Wild flowers are purifiers. He who seeks the wild flowers in their seasons is being directed by the angels, that he might be anointed in a seasonal time."[2]

PICKING DAISIES 1912 (Edgar on right)

…You know, I never can think of anyone being hard hearted, even, or anything else but lovely, who loves flowers.

(464-21) R3 3-11-38

…am a man of the soil but do love beautiful flowers of all kinds,is my real weakness I guess any one can sell me all the flowers can buy
(294) CF 4-17-39

Guess we must be something alike about flowers at least-there is nothing I enjoy more than seeing flowers about the house-and is one of my extravagances for will buy flowers if haven't any for the house every week-wrather do without a sandwich or a smoke than the flowers.

(464) CF 10-8-39)

George Washington Carver was akin to Edgar for he also was humble, loved flowers, and could communicate with the invisible spirit of nature. They had met once and Edgar called him "truly a great soul."[3] Dr. Carver always wore a flower in his buttonhole, and went into the woods every morning at 4 AM to have a talk with God. When asked what it was like to talk to a flower, he said:

How do I talk to a little flower? Through it I talk to the Infinite. And what is the Infinite? It is that silent, small force. It isn't the outer physical contact. No, it isn't that. The Infinite is not confined in the visible world. It is not in the earthquake, the wind or the fire. It is that still small voice that calls up the fairies… Yet, when you look out upon God's beautiful world there it is. When you look into the heart of a rose, there you experience it. But you can't explain it.[4]

Later on, the author said:

I never saw anyone love flowers as Dr. Carver does. Jim Hardwick told me of a walk he once took with him, intending to cover several miles in a few hours. They did not get much farther than a hundred yards. At every little flower he met he had to kneel down. He examined it, caressed it, studied it, talked with it. This love of flowers of Dr. Carver has a lilt about it and a creative, living quality that comes only when love opens up to joy… If you can conceive of the tremendous awe and wonder that one feels when he sees an overwhelming sight like Niagara Falls for the first time, you will understand the feeling that Dr. Carver gets when he looks at a little flower.[5]

Eckhart Tolle speaks of the spiritual aspects of flowers.

> Without our fully realizing it, flowers would become for us an expression in form of that which is most high, most sacred, and utterly formless within ourselves. Flowers, more fleeting, more ethereal, and more delicate than plants out of which they emerged, would become like messengers from another realm, like a bridge between the world of physical forms and the formless. They not only had a scent that was delicate and pleasing to humans, but also brought a fragrance from the realm of spirit. Using the word "enlightenment" in a wider sense than the conventionally accepted one, we could look upon flowers as the enlightenment of plants.[6]
> ...So when you are alert and contemplate a flower, crystal or bird without naming it mentally it becomes a window for you into the formless. There is an inner opening, however slight, into the realm of spirit.[7]
> ...Underneath the surface appearance, everything is not only connected with everything else, but also with the Source of all life out of which it came. Even a stone, and more easily a flower or a bird, could show you the way back to God, to the Source, to yourself. When you look at it or hold it and *let it be* without imposing a word or mental label on it, a sense of awe, of wonder, arises within you. Its essence silently communicates itself to you and reflects your own essence back to you.[8]

Cayce had a great deal to say about flowers. (5122) was told to make them her career, for she had often been a flower lady in past lives.

> Music and flowers, then, should be the entity's work through this experience.
> ...For flowers will love the entity, as the entity loves flowers. Very few would ever find it in themselves to wither while about or on this body.
> ...May we indeed inculcate in the lives of others that like the rose, that like the baby breath, like every flower that blooms. For it does its best with what has been given it by man, to glorify its Maker with all its beauty, its color, with all of its love for the appreciation of spring, of the rain, the sunshine, the shadows.
> ...that man might see His face in the beautiful flowers. Consider the color, the beauty of the lily as it grows from its ugly muck, or the shrinking violet as it sends out its color, its odor to enrich even the very heart of God. Consider the rose as to how it unfolds with the color of the day, and with the opening itself to the sunshine, into the rain.

...For it is in such occasions that flowers should be the companionship of those who are lonely. For they may speak to the "shut-in". They may bring color again to the cheeks of those who are ill. They may bring to the bride the hope of love, of beauty, of a home. For flowers love the places where there is peace and rest. Sunshine and shadows, yes. There are the varied variety from those open fields to those which grow in the bog, but they grow.

(5122-1) T

ROSES
Although Edgar cared about each and every flower, his first love was roses. He had 25 different varieties in his backyard - possibly because they Gertrude loved them so. The rose is queen of the flowers, one of the most sacred associated with love. Its fragrance activates the heart chakra, balances the physical heart, and connects us with the Divine Mother Mary.[9] Ann Ree Colton says, "The rose is the purest flower in the floral kingdom. It is a protective flower creating an atmosphere of purity. It also sanctifies the environment, as the powers of dark cannot come nigh to a pure rose."[10] Edgar's rose poem written in 1912 in Selma, Alabama gives us a glimpse of their world.

EDGAR, GERTRUDE and HUGH LYNN, 1912

I asked the roses as they grew
Richer and lovelier in their
hue
What made their buds so rich
and bright.
They answered –
Looking Toward The Light

One of the first things Edgar planted at 35th street was roses, and for his last garden he ordered Rose of China (Prunus Triloba) from Spring Hill Nursery (ninety cents each). It has double pink flowers that appear before the leaves, blooms until fall and was said to "have few equals." They had a rough start for he planted them too close to the lake where it tended to flood.

> **...have tried to make a bed for some roses, don't know how it will work, where had them was too wet and they died too easily wont get to plant them tho before fall I guess,**
>
> **(464) CF 6-17-35**

> **Sorry your garden was so bad,have had a very nice one here, Vegetables and flowers hadn't had much luck with roses here,guess had put them in too wet a place, so this year I tried fixing a place for them,that would drain well, and they are just looking lovely now although I changed them after they had started to bloom and got others also, they seem to have taken on new life and a very pretty.ordered some slips of course expected to get as ordered different colors but seems they sent me all red Roses like red but would like to have had some of them different,But the Larkspur,Petunias, Pansies,Touch me not. Zenia, Nastursians,Cosmos, Gladiolas.and a few others have been lovely all year or season and all are still very pretty. my Phlox have just begun to look pretty but make a very pretty back ground against the house.**
>
> **(464) CF 8-20-35**

Whenever he travelled, he would visit the roses.

> Oh the flowers in some of the places were beautiful – in Texas were in the Rose center – and there were acres and acres of gorgeous roses –

and the fields full of the Primrose all colors and the same in La. and
Ala. There the flowers were all a bloom of ever description – just
loved them.

(1770-4) R22 5-31-40

One flower that Edgar always wanted but couldn't afford was a tuberose
with a spike of creamy white lily-like flowers. Although it has rose in its
name, it is related to the amaryllis family. It promotes serenity and peace
of mind, increases sensitivity and psychic abilities, and has strong
energies of love and attraction. A common superstition was that its
fragrance was the odor of death, and if you smelled it in a closed room
you would die.[11]

A long time I have been wishing for some bulbs of tube roses. To me
they are very desirable, but owing to the high price most of the
nurseries put on them I've never been able to get hold of any. But the
other day a man came in with some chickens from the country. [Mr.
Dozier?] He saw where I had been digging around in the ground. He
said, "I see you are fixing for some flowers, Dr. Cayce." I said, "Yes, I
love flowers." "So do I," he replied. "I live way down in the country,
and I always have every sort of thing. I have one thing I would like to
bring you, if you care for them. Do you like tube roses?" So, at last I
have a little bunch of tube roses, that may be really beautiful. Don't
you like them? We wish for it, we pray for it, we try to live it – and in
His time He sees fit that we may have it. This, I am sure, applies to
material things, to spiritual things, to our mental abilities.

(464-12) R31 3-8-33

Yes, it is very easy to associate flowers that are so fragrant as the
tuberose with certain experiences in our lives. The tuberose has always
reminded me of a funeral, but since I have come to look at death in a
much different way than formerly I look at such now rather as a birth,
or possibility, than as so much separation. Rather as an opportunity for
expansion of whatever may have been builded by the individual, than
a cutting off.

(464-13) R7 3-20-33

VIOLETS
Sweet violets were Edgar's second favorite flower that miraculously
survived being transplanted three times and happily bloomed throughout
the winter for him.

The last year I have been moving around considerable, and such things, you know, can't just be pulled up and set down anywhere and be expected to do anything; so practically the only thing I've saved out of all the beautiful assortment is my violets. They have been moved so often that I suppose when they see anyone coming with a hoe they wonder where they're going next. They are very appreciative, and if given the opportunity they bloom forth with all their might and main, and raise those beautiful heads with all the fragrance that is theirs alone to give. They are blooming beautifully now, and will no doubt continue until next June, as they have done since I have had them.

(464-12) R23 10-21-32

…We rarely have freezes for longer than a day at a time; rarely have much snow; consequently such blossoms as the violets rather thrive in the character of weather we have.

(464-12) R25 11-16-32

We have had a very quiet but pleasant Christmas. The Day here was mild – the temperature. Our sweet violets were all in bloom; we had a little boquet sitting on my desk.

(464) CF 12-27-32

Violets have a very high vibration, respond to prayer, and help us attune to the fairies and elves. Legend says it is sacred to the Fairy Queen, and picking the first wild spring violet brings the assistance of the fairies to fulfill one's dearest wish in the coming year.[12] "When one feels attracted to flowers yielding a velvet moisture in their petals, [violets] he has a grace aspect from the lunar or moon cycles. He is ardent, tender and inclined toward a pure mystical reverence."[13]

They were the favorite flower of "Little Anna", a childhood friend that Edgar met and adored when she was five and he was four. They had a short, magical friendship of only eighteen months when his family moved once again. She, too, could speak with the flowers, trees, fairies, elves and invisible playmates and be a part of his world. They played in the woods, barn and churchyard where the violets grew wild. In the summertime they chased dragonflies and collected violets, and caught snowflakes in their mouths in the winter.

In 1939 when Cayce was 62, Mr. (1861) requested a reading, and nine months later his fiancée (2072) also wanted one. Even before they met, Edgar recognized them as "Little Anna" and her father who had reincarnated and were together again. In his letters he went back to the happiest time of his life.

> …but can be still and listen to a something deep within and easily
> imagine am listening to little Anna again, as we played by the spring,
> or the hay rick or in the garden with the little playmates or walked
> through the fields of grain careful to walk with the rows so as not to
> disturb the growing and ripening grain – for each head of grain were
> alive to us and the little folk, with a message of thought and care of
> God for the children of men, in same, preparing food for bodily
> growth.
>
> (2072-2) R8 12-31-40

She asked Edgar how to meditate, and he said to imagine a deep purple
cardboard with a hole and a candle behind it.

> Yes – we used it [the cardboard] when we used to play together, do
> not know that it was the little folk who told us, or was just chance –
> but we used it first to play house for we always played we were
> keeping house together – we were the little home builders right.
> …The school where we went was just across the road from the Church.
> We played in the Church yard and the wood around same, and there
> were more pretty Violets in that wood – they must still be your
> favorite flower – for they were then and many the day you had your
> little arms full of them – literally, will tell you something of them
> when you are here this time.
>
> (2072-6) R6 2-25-42

> Been a long time since have had any thing that was as much pleasure
> as having you here - makes me think of the times we had together –
> the Hay Rick – Barn on the island, at Circus and one or two days at
> school, and just lose myself in dreaming when allow myself to dream
> like that – and wish to have you all to myself again as then.
>
> (2072-6) R10 3-11-42

She and her father had died of pneumonia in 1891. Edgar, who was
fourteen, walked a long way through the snow to be at her bedside.

> If my memory serves me right – and it may not it was Feb. of 87 or 88
> will never forget the experience – for felt something was taken
> from me – and walked several miles myself to be with you at the end.
>
> (2072-2) R2 7-10-40

It was a devastating loss for Edgar in many ways. The "little people" stopped coming, and his dead grandfather, who had visited him in the barn almost daily for ten years, never came again.

ENDNOTES

1-Colton, Ann Ree *Watch Your Dreams* p. 184-5
2-Ibid p. 187
3-Letter to 1387 from Edgar Cayce. (294) CF 6-12-43
4-Clark, Glenn *The Man Who Talks With The Flowers* p. 44-45
5-Ibid p. 40-2
6-Tolle, Eckhart *The New Earth* p. 2-3
7-Ibid p. 5
8-Ibid p. 25-6
9-Andrews, Ted *Nature Speak* p. 360
10-Colton p. 186
11-Ibid p. 366
12-Ibid p. 368-9
13-Ibid p. 186

PLUM TREES IN BLOSSOM
Spring 2009
A.R.E.

Chapter Seven
JAM, "SUGAR SHOWERS" AND VEGETABLES

Now I have a few beans, radishes, some corn, tomatoes, okra, squash,
and a few things like that, which to me - at least - appears to be
a great deal better when fresh.   (464-13) R12 5-15-33

JAM AND "SUGAR SHOWERS"

Edgars garden also included the wild Scuppernaug grapes that grew over
the sand hills. He would pick them by the bushel and make grape jelly.
Later on he was able to have his own grape vines and make not only
grape, but peach and pear jelly as well. He was always canning and
preserving the bountiful harvests that he loved to share, and his
masterpieces were brandied peaches, peach pickle and fig jam.

> ...I sent yesterday a little package for you.   It isn't much, but you
> may enjoy seeing and tasting it; though I don't know how well you
> like fig preserves.   We have a great many figs in this district.   I don't
> know as you know it, but I have prided myself on being able to make
> good fig preserves.   Now, these were made by my own hands; no,
> the Madam didn't watch them nor measure out anything, nor have
> anything to do with them.   So, if they are not good, the fault is all my
> own.   I don't know what gives me such a peculiar twist, but I don't
> know of anything I like better than making preserves or jellies of any
> kind – I love to just fool with it!   I felt that possibly you would like
> this, and I hope you will enjoy it very much.
>
> (325) CF 9-21-32

> ...I still do the bigger part of the preserving here, from choice – to
> be sure. Muddie [Gertrude] would do it if I didn't, but it's one of my
> hobbies I guess.   I'm laughed at sometimes for it, but who cares – if
> you can make somebody laugh it's fine!   I've made more apple jelly
> from the cores and peelings than we have had for some time; also
> prepared quite a number of jars of apples for apple "sass [sauce]" a
> little later on.
> ...I have three pint jars of fig preserves, the prettiest that I have
> ever made – and for one who feels he is a connoisseur in such things,
> why that's saying right smart!   I hope to get some grapes and enough
> of the wild kind that grow around here to make a little wine,

inasmuch as I think we are doing away with prohibition.

(2457) CF 8-10-33

...I've done a great deal more preserving, canning, jellying and pickling than I have in a long time; in fact, since I was in Selma. I canned and preserved a bushel of peaches. Then when I went to making pickle I struck some very <u>lovely</u> clingstone peaches and I have pickled and preserved about a bushel of those. Then, canning about fourteen to sixteen gallons of apples (for apple sauce) enabled me to make a great deal of jelly also. I haven't known anything about canning vegetables. I just got hold of a good recipe after all my beans were gone; I could have had several gallons of beans because we had to throw them away. Tomatoes have also been more than plentiful. We have given away several bushels. I remember Mother used to can tomatoes, but they are so hard to keep __ and then they are really so cheap, good brands of them even, that I don't know that it really pays.

(482) CF 8-27-35

Peach pickle is an old southern favorite and the recipe was handed down from generation to generation. Young clingstones are the best variety and must be peeled. A bushel weighs about 50 pounds. There are several internet recipes with similar ingredients.

Nana's Southern Pickled Peaches [1]

4 cups sugar
1 cup white vinegar
1 cup water
2 tablespoons whole cloves
4 pounds fresh clingstone peaches, blanched and peeled
5 (3 inch) cinnamon sticks

Combine the sugar, vinegar and water in a large pot, and bring to a boil.
Boil for 5 minutes. Press one or two cloves into each peach, and place into the boiling syrup. Boil for 20 minutes, or until peaches are tender.

Spoon peaches into sterile jars and top with liquid to ½ inch from the rim.
Put one cinnamon stick into each jar. Wipe the rims with a clean dry

cloth, and seal with lids and rings. Process in a hot water bath for 10 minutes to seal, or consult times recommended by your local extension.

By the next summer Edgar had learned to can vegetables, and create combinations for soup.

> ...but when you talk about preserving and Jelly, Apple sauce and like well that is my hobby, my wife thinks I am crazy at times but find it is all mighty good when the bad days come on. but for Aplle sauce the two boys here and the Secy I think could eat a quart every day, they are very fond of it, have put up quite a bit of that think the last I made yesterday made about 16 Gal in all and jelly well guess have enough of that to last for several years, I like when our friends come in to give them a glass of Jelly and all say I am a pretty good hand at it.havent ben able to get any Crabb apples would like a bit of that.and as for Raspberries we have so few of those round here, and are too expensive to buy to put up. have been trying my hand this year with a few vegetables putting   Beans Butter beans Okra Corn and Tomatoes together for Soup this winter. have about 10 out of that,I like to work with peaches also,am waiting now for the cling stone to make Pickle, am very fond of that and most of the others are also.guess will have some of those next week
> ...one of my well they are not patients,but one that has had quite a success with his reading, brought me two bushels of grapes yesterday,had a job working them up, but made wine of most of them, so guess that will be alright by next summer or in two years or such a matter any way, will want to get a few pears,like them with a few grapes with them best, and a few nuts,that is the only way they are good to me,
>
> (464) CF 8-19-36

Since sugar was rationed in war-time, his friends gave him "sugar showers" so he would have enough.

> ...will soon as can get hold of a box send more jelly-had a sugar shower this week so have enough to make some more if didnt have,some already,dont know about jars might cost as much to return old ones as it would to get new ones,but you can see if you get hold of a container-but will send some along any way in next day or so. Glad you liked it. and that the others found it good-that is a great complement and makes me anxious to get more to you-that is what

it is made for-and it likes to get eaten up.

(487) CF 9-17-42

…have been very fortunate about sugar- many of the group gave me a sugar shower other night so have a nice lot to make into jelly and jams now.

(2635) CF 9-18-42

Our strawberries have been very nice, but I don't have time to gather them.   Someone, Miss Mary [Mary Wirsing?] I believe, went out and gathered a pan full the other morning.   We made them into preserves.   Only three pints when we had enough for three gallons if we could have gotten them picked and had the sugar.

(2072-14) R4 5-26-44

VEGETABLES
The readings emphasized the importance of fresh, local food with high life force energy.

…In the noon, there may be those of the vegetables that are fresh, and as are ESPECIALLY grown in the vicinity where the body resides. Shipped vegetables are never very good.

(2-14) T

…Do not have large quantities of any fruits, vegetables, meats, that are not grown in or come to the area where the body is at the time it partakes of such foods.   This will be found to be a good rule to be followed by all.   This prepares the system to acclimate itself to any given territory.

(3542-1) T

…As it is so well advertised that coffee loses its value in fifteen to twenty to twenty-five days after being roasted, so do foods or vegetables lose their food value after being gathered - in the same proportion in hours as coffee would in days.

(340-31) T

Edgar followed the recommendation in the readings to have more above ground green leafy vegetables, for he grew spinach, mustard and turnip greens which are full of minerals and nutrients, especially calcium. Too many below ground vegetables at a meal can bring our energy down.

DO have plenty of vegetables above the ground; at least three of these to one below the ground. Have at least one leafy vegetable to every one of the pod vegetables taken.

(2602-1) T

*EDGAR'S GARDEN VEGETABLES

ABOVE GROUND
Artichoke (globe)
*Asparagus
*Bean
Broccoli
Brussel Sprout
*Cabbage
Cauliflower
Celery
*Corn (technically a grain)
Cucumber
Eggplant
Leafy Greens
*Lettuce
Mushroom
*Mustard Greens
*Okra
*Pea
Pepper
*Poke
*Pumpkin
Rutabaga
*Spinach
*Squash
*Tomato
*Turnip Greens

BELOW GROUND
*Beet
*Carrot
Garlic
Ginger
*Jerusalem Artichoke
Kohlrabi
Leek
*Onion
Parsnip
*Potato
*Radish
*Salsify
*Turnip

In May 1943, his sister Annie had moved and was planning another garden, so Edgar told her how to plant strawberries and asparagus. His letter, unfortunately, was illegible in two places.

Set out strawberries in early spring–or that is when I have found it best. Asparagus bed-have always made mine the old fashioned way Dig a bed about three feet wide and as long as you want it–dig down about tw and half feet put rock and cinder in bottom say about a foot of it then soil up to about [??] inches of top, then burn the dirt [??] ills to top burn pretty hard, set the roots about where you put the burnt dirt.

then burn off each spring after the 2nd year gets better each year ours this year we have asparagus every other day,and all we can eat–with enough to give others some now and then.

...Well have to go put up my peas have been trying my hand at canning a few dont know whether will work or not never tried any,put up three pints so far,now have a few more,

(243) CF 5-27-43

An 1888 farmers encyclopedia[2] explained that the soil was burned to give asparagus (a marine plant) salt and alkalies for fertilizer. Burning the the dead stalks with any loose dry material in the spring furnished what was needed to improve the beds for years. The Romans also burned "the haulm in its own place". The encyclopedia helped with the missing information in the first illegible place in the letter, for it said the soil was to be three inches from the top. After being planted ,the roots were covered with rich soil, a peck of ashes and a peck of salt all mixed together. If grown near the seacoast, it was not necessary to add salt.

SALAD
Cayce highly recommended a raw salad almost every day for lunch to keep the pH alkaline, kill parasites, stimulate the immune system, purify the blood, and help maintain regular eliminations.

(Q)　How did the trouble of pin worms originate,　or what caused it?
(A)　Milk!　You see, in every individual there is within the intestinal tract that matter which produces a form of intestinal worm.　This is in everyone.　But with a particular diet where the milk has any bacillus,　it will gradually cause these to increase, and they oftentimes develop or multiply rapidly;　and then they may

disappear, IF there is taken raw, green food.

(Q) Would you change the kind of milk she drinks?
(A) It isn't so much the change in the kind of milk that is needed.
Either add the raw, green foods as indicated, or give those
properties as would eliminate the sources of same. But it is better,
if it is practical, to induce the body to eat lettuce and celery and
carrots, - even a small amount. One leaf of lettuce will destroy a
thousand worms.

(2015-10) T

A young woman who was travelling to Europe was concerned about
staying healthy without shots.

(Q) Are inoculations against contagious diseases necessary for me
before sailing in September? [from N.Y. to England and Scotland]
(A) As we find, only where the requirements are such as to
DEMAND same would this be adhered to at all. So far as the
body-physical condition is concerned, the adherence to the use of
carrots, lettuce and CELERY EVERY day at a meal or as a portion of
the meal will insure against any contagious infectious forces with
which the body may be in contact.

(Q) Can immunization against them be set up in any other manner
than by inoculation?
(A) As indicated, if an alkalinity is maintained in the system –
especially with lettuce, carrots and celery, these in the blood supply
will maintain such a condition as to immunize a person.

(480-19) T

A 56 year old woman with colitis tendencies wanted to know about
lettuce.

(Q) Should plenty of lettuce be eaten?
(A) Plenty of lettuce should always be eaten by most EVERY body;
for this supplies an effluvium [an invisible vapor] in the blood
stream itself that is a destructive force to MOST of those influences
that attack the blood stream. It's a purifier.

(404-6) T

The temptation is to take our vegetables in pill form for convenience,
but Cayce preferred them fresh.

(Q)   It is difficult for me to arrange one daily meal of salad only; therefore, might I supplement my diet by tablets recommended by Dr. Black, taking one tablet daily each of SODEOM, WEST'S VEGETABLE TABLETS, AND SEALAX?

(A)   These may be taken if there is a lack of those activities from the raw salad; but they do not, WILL not, supply the energies as well or as efficaciously for the BODY as if there were the efforts made to have at least one meal each day altogether of raw vegetables, or two meals carrying raw salad as a portion of same – each day.

(1158-1) T

It is healthy not only to dig in the dirt, but to eat a little dirt along with the vegetables, for it supplies the colon with beneficial soil organisms.

…It is well for people, individuals, as this entity, to get their hands dirty in the dirt at times, and not be the white-collared man all the while!   These are natural sources.   From whence was man made? Don't be afraid to get a little dirt on you once in a while.   You know you must eat a certain amount of dirt, else you'll never get well balanced.   For this is that from which all conditions arise.   For of dust man is made, and to dust he returns.

(3352-1) T

A 40 year old woman with a fracture of the femur that had not healed after a year was told to eat clean sand or dirt found in the sun near a river, and more below ground vegetables.

…What is needed is the vibration or the radiation from ground, earth, soil in the body – even a little sand or dirt taken would be well for this body.   While there should not be used that which is soiled by any excesses, but that which is in the sunlight, sand close to the riverways.   Just three to four to five grains – that means by weight, not just grains of sand.   It would be well for this to be eaten with the food, or on the food.

(3608-1) T

Although Edgar grew potatoes, the readings advised that only the mineral rich, nutritious skins be eaten.

Then as to the diet: Add to the diet the Irish potato PEEL, but not the pulp a great deal.   It would be better if the nice potatoes are cleansed, peeled and only the PEELINGS cooked and eaten! Throw the other part away, or give it to the chickens, or distribute it in some other manner besides eating it!

(1904-1) T

A few unusual vegetables were mentioned in the readings that may have been grown at Arctic Crescent where there was more land.

JERUSALEM ARTICHOKE (Helianthus tuberosus, Fam. Asteraceae) (Girasole, Sunchoke, Sunflower artichoke, Potatoes of Canada) is a seven to fifteen foot tall member of the sunflower family. Its edible tuber was cultivated for food by the Indians. Since one tuber spreads and produces numerous plants, it is best to grow them in a separate area of the garden. They do not keep well and should be left in the ground until ready to use, preferably after a frost. Putting a bale of hay over them in colder climates keeps the ground from freezing, thus making an easy harvest. Cayce said to use them fresh (not dried) for diabetes, for they contain inulin, a natural form of insulin that stabilizes blood sugar. One tuber the size of a hen's egg can be eaten raw in a salad, or cooked in Patapar Paper[3] two or three times a week.

They should be taken under the supervision of a physician for they may alter the need for oral medicine or insulin. A 70 year old man with diabetes asked:

(Q) What was the Jerusalem artichoke given for?
(A) An activity upon the pancreas. It carries – it is the greatest source of insulin that may be assimilated by the body.

(2094-2) T

A 66 year old woman who had a "light case of diabetes which I control with n40 insulin once a day"[4] was advised:

Instead of using so much insulin; this can be gradually diminished and eventually eliminated entirely if there is used in the diet one Jerusalem artichoke every other day. This should be cooked only in Patapar paper, preserving the juices and mixing with the bulk of the artichoke, seasoning this to suit the taste. The taking of insulin is habit forming. The artichoke is not habit forming,…

(4023-1) T

They were also given for people with a tendency for diabetes such as

Mrs. (3386) who was overweight and loved sweets.

(Q)   Craving for sweets?
(A)   This is natural with the indigestion and the lack of proper activity of the pancreas.   Eat a Jerusalem artichoke once each week, about the size of a hen egg.   Cook this in Patapar paper, preserving all the juices to mix with the bulk of the artichoke.   Season to taste. This will also aid in the disorder in the circulation between liver and kidneys, pancreas and kidneys, and will relieve these tensions from the desire for sweets.

(3386-2) T

POKE (Phytolacca decandra [LINN.] N.O. Phytolaccaceae)
(Pocan, Pigeon Berry, Poke Berry, Poke Root, Poke Weed, Polk, Red-ink plant, Virginian Poke) grows wild and shows up everywhere. It would have loved the vibrations of Edgar's garden, and chickens eat the deep purple berries. "This is regarded as one of the most important of indigenous American plants and one of the most striking in appearance…The young (spring) shoots make a good substitute for asparagus."[5] Cayce said poke was a blood purifier and cleanser, and *should be gathered ONLY when the shoots are very young – between 4 to 6 inches.*[6] Very specific directions were given for their preparation because all parts of poke are poisonous. After surgery for breast cancer, a 56 year old woman was told to eat poke, drink plantain tea, and eat one almond a day.

…Eat very young poke – the tender shoots of the pokeweed – to act as a purifier for the body.
Prepare it in this manner: When cutting sufficient [*4 to 6 inches*] to make a small dish or salad, put in cold water and let come to a boil. Strain or drain off, as in a colander – or put in a colander and let all the juice drain off.   Then prepare or cook the remaining leaves with other greens, especially such as lamb's- tongue and wild mustard – about an equal quantity. This eaten once a week will purify the whole body.

(3515-1) T

SALSIFY (Tragopogon porrifolius [LINN.] N.O. Compositae)
(Oyster Plant, Purple Goats Beard, Salsafy, Vegetable Oyster) is a long, tapered cream colored root that contains gold, iodine, silicon, calcium, phosphorous, iron, salts and vitamins. It also does not keep well when harvested and is best left in the ground until needed. It is easy to grow,

but manure should be avoided for it causes the root to fork.

> "To serve plain boiled, the roots must be scraped lightly first, cut up into two or three portions, and placed in water, with a few drops of lemon juice or vinegar, to prevent them discolouring. Then boiled for an hour, quickly, in salt water until tender, drained and served with white sauce."[7]

Cayce frequently recommended it for the gold has anti-aging properties, the salts prevent and eliminate hardening of the tendons, and the vitamins and minerals are easily assimilated. It should be cooked in Patapar Paper to save the salts and nutrients. A twelve year old boy with severe asthma wanted to know why his thumbnails had ridges, and was told to eat foods that are high in calcium.

> (Q) What causes the deep ridges in thumbnail and what treatments should be followed?
> (A) These are the activities of the glandular force, and the addition of those foods which carry large quantities of calcium will make for bettered conditions in this direction. Take often chicken neck, chew it. Cook this well, the feet and those portions of the fowl, and we will find it will add calcium to the body. Also eat bones of fish, as in canned fish. Also parsnips and oyster plant; all of these, of course, in their regular season. Wild game of any kind, but chew the bones of same. All of these will be well for the body.
>
> (5192-1) T

ENDNOTES

1-Internet recipe

2-The National Farmers and Housekeepers Cyclopaedia, FM Lupton Publisher, 1888 p. 87

3-Patapar Paper is parchment paper that may be used fifty times. Wet it, place one vegetable in the

  middle, tie it up and place the bag in boiling water. Length of cooking time varies. Rinse after use

  and hang to dry. Available at A.R.E. Bookstore (See appendix for address)

4-(4023-1) B1 7-27-43

5-Grieve, Mrs. M. *A Modern Herbal Volume II (I-Z)* p. 648

6-Thomas, Jeanette M. *The Edgar Cayce Plant Encyclopedia Volume I* p. 168

7-Grieve p. 709

ARE
Edgar's Fig Trees
Spring 2008

Chapter Eight

THIRD GARDEN – CAYCE HOSPITAL –
105th St and Atlantic Ave June 1928-February 1931
FOURTH GARDEN –
105th St and Oceanfront June 1931-February 1932
FIFTH GARDEN –
403 Lake Drive March 1932-April 1932

Aid others in appreciating the beauty, - even of mud, of snow, of nature, of trees,or the ability to communicate one with another; the meaningsof home, of environment, of peace, of harmony.   (2404-1) T

THIRD GARDEN

Edgar's third garden was at the Cayce Hospital for Research and Enlightenment at 105th Street (later renamed 67th Street) and Atlantic Avenue. In 1911 he had been guided to build an institution in Virginia Beach, and eighteen years later it became a reality. Any beach has healing forces from the sun, salt and sea breeze, but the sand there is unique for it contains gold and radium. The five acre property on both sides of Atlantic Avenue had a 30 bed hospital and educational center with a library, lecture hall, tennis courts, croquet, shuffleboard and a twelve car garage. Ground was broken June, 1928, and Edgar worked side by side with the carpenters and gardener. He was extremely busy but found time to plant his roses and violets on the front and south side of the hospital for everyone to enjoy. "One of the patients on leaving the hospital, feeling wonderful, was presented with a boquet of violets gathered from the flower bed in the side of the yard."1. His vision for the grounds included a sunken meditation garden on the west of the hospital (now a staff parking lot), but the depression hit and the hospital closed before it could be implemented. Two eighty year old fig trees he planted on the east side of the carriage house, and two plum trees (age?) by the driveway are still productive. The branches of the plum trees are covered with lichen, and one trunk measures forty-five inches in diameter.

Shortly after the hospital opened February 11, 1929, Edgar reported to (900):

> The grounds are beginning to look real good. This we have had to spend a lot of money on, but – as you said sometime ago – we don't

want to spoil the whole thing by being penny wise and pound follish [foolish] respecting this part of the work.

(900-422) R5 2-20-29

They spent even more money than estimated, however, because the eastern slope of the sand dune washed out badly in a heavy rainfall and had to be landscaped into terraces with $10,000 worth of sod.

TERRACES, no sod, January 1929

TERRACES, with sod, Christmas 1929

Edgar's mother died October 25, 1926, and a fountain (a nine foot circle with a figure in the center pouring water) was built in her memory in front of the hospital. Another fountain was built on the same site in 2005. (ch. 10)

LESLIE CAYCE (Edgar's father)
AT FOUNTAIN DEDICATION, 1929

The hospital had a waiting list, but Edgar was not a business man and would not charge for a reading if someone could not pay. The stock market crash caused more financial difficulties, and two years after it opened, the Blumenthals withdrew their financial support from both the hospital and Edgar personally. As if that wasn't enough, two months later they evicted him from his home; a place he believed was his - where he had poured his heart into the garden.

...Then to have them all taken away again seemed like something was wrong; for each of those trees, plants and rosebushes seemed to have a message for me from time to time.

(464-12) R27 12-1-32

FOURTH GARDEN

In September 1930, Edgar rented a fourteen room Wright Cottage at 105th Street and Oceanfront (now 6610 67th Street) for a friend who was invited to move to Virginia Beach and run it as a hotel for hospital visitors. Things didn't work out as planned, and Edgar still held the lease when he was evicted. Even though he fortunately had a place to go to on such short notice, it was not the best location, for he was constantly reminded of his loss.

...It's a big house, but we really haven't as much room as we had at 35th Street.   We are at 105th Street on the ocean, the house right in front of the hospital.   I suppose everybody will think that we haven't any sentiment, or do love to punish ourselves if we have any sentiment whatsoever.

(2457) CF 7-9-31

WRIGHT COTTAGE, 1976 – postcard

It was an extremely difficult time. He was depressed, felt responsible for the loss of the hospital and had health problems. He didn't even try to start another garden, but spent a great deal of time meditating with the few roses and violets that he had saved.

Many thanks for the flowers.   We have some violets blooming in the yard – they have been since the latter part of November, although we are really just a stone's throw from the ocean.

(2457) CF 1-12-32

Ten months later, Blumenthal purchased the Wright Cottage, refused to renew Edgar's lease and forced him to move again the end of February, 1932.

FIFTH GARDEN

This time he found two tiny cottages close together at 403 Lake Drive in the Pinewood section at the southern end of Lake Holly. One was used as their home and the other was an office where Gladys and her sister Mildred lived.

OFFICE COTTAGE, March or April 1932
Left to right – Gladys, Leslie B. Cayce, Edgar, Gertrude

It was springtime and things were looking up. Edgar was feeling better and transplanted his roses, violets and chickens for the second time.

> One would never suspect by looking out the window now that they were any ways near the ocean, for we have trees and leaves, gravel road and mud, instead of sand, that is, mud when it rains, also we are only about four or five minutes' walk from the ocean.
> …Now, I have got to stop here again. This is only a very little note, but I hear some of my little chickens calling me.
>
> (2123-1) R7 3-14-32

He even counted how many steps it took to reach the ocean!

> …We are opposite 11th and 12th, were they able to run on through – but just off of the boulevard about a block, after crossing the railroad you come to a fresh water lake. We are on the other side of the lake. If we had a bridge completed across the lack, we would not be more than two or three minutes from the ocean. As it is, we are only five hundred and twenty-one steps from the ocean. Mr. L.B. and the family live in the house on the lake. Nearly a block up the street Miss Gladys, Mildred and Gray are staying – in the place where we have the offices, and where also I have my chickens and work shop. It was here that I "petered" out while building the chicken house. Remember when we built the garage on 35th Street? [ch. 5]
>
> (2457) CF 3-16-32

Hugh Lynn immediately started another flower garden, but the move had been hard on the chickens.

> My chickens, I think, have a much better place than I ever had. We have killed our chickens off to about two dozen or a little more, but are getting about enough eggs to supply the table. The move broke up most of those that wanted to set; possibly most of our chickens other than the 30 that we have will be late.
> Hugh Lynn has taken in a corner in front of the little woods house, (you know we have two houses, the lake house and the woods house) and has laid out an old fashioned flower garden which should be very pretty when it comes along in shape.
>
> (294) CF 3-23-32

It was quite a new experience to be on a lake farther away from the beach and he loved it.

I think we are all liking our change better and better while it was very lovely to be close to the ocean, [105th & Ocean, later numbered 67th St.] yet to be close to nature, to God's trees and His birds is wonderful also, and we are only a three or four minutes' walk from the ocean. I am hoping you will have the opportunity to make us a visit while we are here. It is quite different surroundings from anything we have experienced since we have been in Virginia, yet we really like it in a way that I hope will enable us to do better service for the Master.

(428-5) R3 3-25-32

There are many things for, and possibly a few against, our present location. We are not quite so close to the sea. The dwelling is on a beautiful little lake, that comes up right in the back yard. It is fresh water, and we may stand in the back yard and also see the ocean down the street – about a four and a half minutes walk from the house. The other place, where the young ladies live – and where we have the offices – is a little farther up the street – graveled street, but very nice sidewalks – and the building is in the edge of a very pretty wood. A little distance away there are some very beautiful pine groves. Having been in Virginia Beach several years, and not having lived except where we could step out in the sand, we haven't gotten used to being here where there is clay and mud, and when it rains – unless we have a little grass or sidewalk – it's just too bad! But having the woods and the flowers, seems to me to make us able to combine more of God's blessings in this little vicinity. It will enable us to have a little vegetable garden, which we couldn't do very well before. Then, too, we were able to get these two little places at a much cheaper rate – which is a very necessary adjunct under the existent conditions. But we have SO MUCH to be thankful for, we should praise God more and more. He from whom blessings flow!

(2123-1) R10 3-28-32

There was a glitch in cheaper paradise, however. Edgar had rented a property that was for sale on the condition that he would vacate when it sold. His luck ran out immediately.

Yes, today is a very beautiful day here also. It makes one feel like getting Out and digging around the flowers, but we have had such

nice luck, I don't know Whether I feel like digging, cussing or praying – I guess I need to pray.   We have only been here, you know, just a month, in fact, on the 29th day that we were here we were notified that one of the places had been sold, so we must begin to look for another place, and we had done considerable work in clearing up, had dug us up a garden space, though we had not put any seed in.   We had laid out a beautiful flower garden at the little woods house.   It will be pretty for somebody, so it's possibly not all lost, anyway.   Don't know just yet what we will do.
…I am afraid my chickens will be like the old fellow's that every time the wagon drove up they ran and to stick up their feet to be tied.   The trouble is, I don't know whether I will be able to have them at any place that we may go.   Of course, there are many places that we couldn't.   I have five hens setting now and thirty chicks the size of a partridge, or a little bigger.

(2457) CF 4-7-32

   Yes, Hugh Lynn's flower bed is coming up beautifully.   We are just in the edge of the woods where there is beautiful dogwood, red buds, honeysuckle, mayapple, violets – all in bloom, to say nothing of the sweet violets we have put around the house.   Everything is coming fine. The lady who came to look at the house the other day said, "Well, maybe you can thank the good Lord that somebody will enjoy it."   We do!

(2457) CF 4-22-32

Two weeks later he found a rental on the north end of the same lake. His dream of finally owning another home eventually came true when he was able to purchase it in 1936 and have a permanent place for his garden.

…I think I wrote you that we were having such a hard time getting ourselves located. We moved from 35th Street to the one I hoped you would occupy, and found that was just too expensive for us.   We gave it up the first of March and moved into two small cottages at the other end of the beach.   In thirty days, after I had done quite a bit of fixing up around, one of the places was sold – and now we have to be on the move again.   We have tentatively made arrangements for a place.   I know the location is not as desirable as some might be, yet it will be quite alright I am sure.   Then, if we move there, we will be across the street from the Catholic Church. I hope we can make the deal.   If we do, we will be buying the place at what we would be paying for rent anywhere else.   Then if we could keep up the payments, or rent, in a few years we would at least have some equity in the place and will not have to be bothered with having to move so often without any prospects of a return.

(294) CF 5-5-32

CATHOLIC CHURCH (right) EDGAR'S HOME (left), 1943

It was Edgar's deep, abiding faith in God that enabled him to survive such overwhelming loss of the hospital, his home, garden and two moves in one year without becoming bitter. A few months after moving for the last time, he wrote down his thoughts on patience, adversity, prayer and surrender.

July the last, 1932

Patience
    Cultivating the soil in which
the Soul grows.
    submitting to Gods plans
for us.   Praying when the
things that so easily next assail us
    Loving indifference to
trial and tribulation
an active force against petty worries.
    Recognizing God plan with
others.   by not judging others
not criticizing others.
    Keep our own emotions pure
in the light of our own understading.

Patience.
    Chief cornerstone in Soul
building.
    Seeing good in the worst
of every other ones faulet
    Crucifying selfishness
doing our bit to make
Jesus promises Real in other
peoples lives.
    Blessing them that speak evil
of our attempts to do good for others
    Loving our enemies.
looking for the good in
our fellow man
giving thanks for Bounty
giving praise adversity
    Keeping joyous in the work
of the Lord.

ENDNOTES

1-Gladys'summary of the Cayce Hospital events, November 18,

Edgar's Flowers

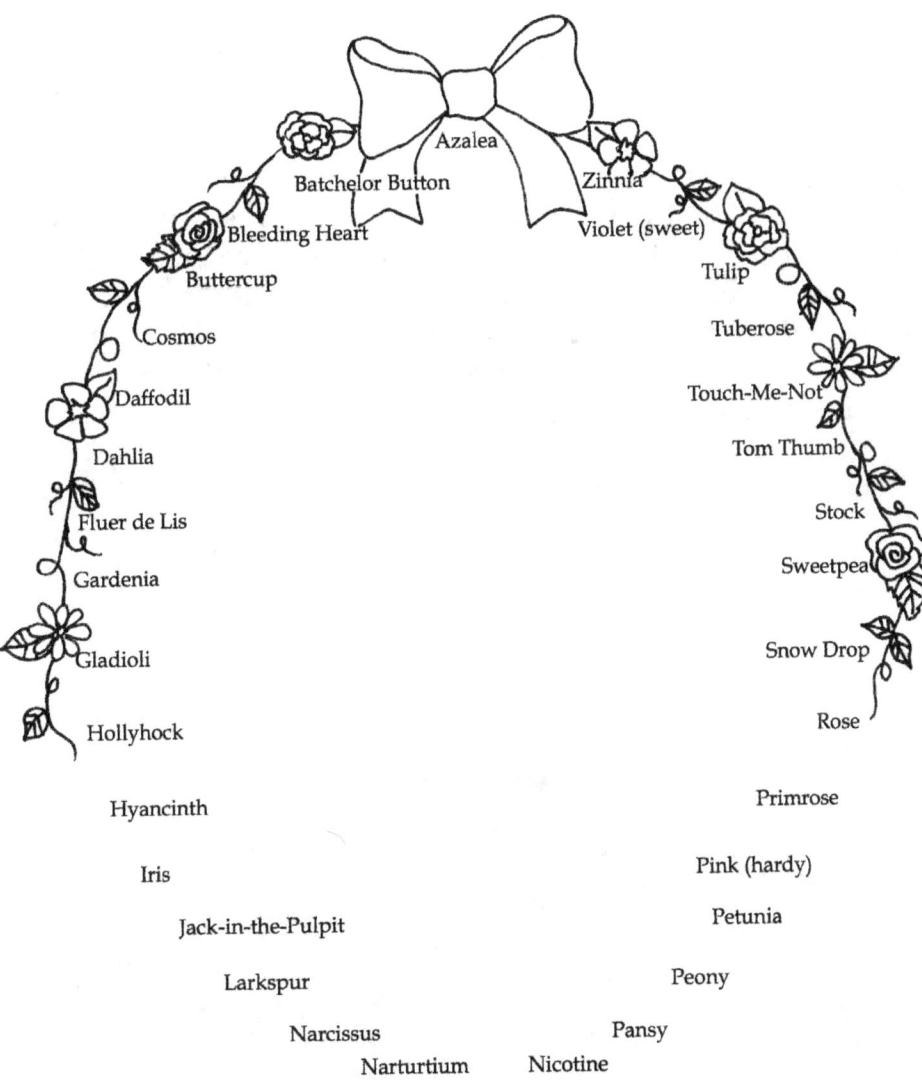

Azalea

Batchelor Button

Bleeding Heart

Buttercup

Cosmos

Daffodil

Dahlia

Fluer de Lis

Gardenia

Gladioli

Hollyhock

Hyancinth

Iris

Jack-in-the-Pulpit

Larkspur

Narcissus

Narturtium

Zinnia

Violet (sweet)

Tulip

Tuberose

Touch-Me-Not

Tom Thumb

Stock

Sweetpea

Snow Drop

Rose

Primrose

Pink (hardy)

Petunia

Peony

Pansy

Nicotine

Chapter Nine

SIXTH GARDEN - 308 Arctic Crescent
May 1932 – January 1945

...he who understands nature walks close with God.   (1904-2) T

All of Edgar's homes were within two blocks of the ocean, and the last two were on Lake Holly, a fairly large fresh water lake. Edgar moved to the DeTreville house May, 1932, a spacious summer cottage at 308 Arctic Crescent near 14th street and Pacific Avenue. It was a block away from Star of the Sea Catholic Church and the local jail. His roses, violets and a few flowers were moved one last time, but – as he had feared – there was no room for the chickens.

308 ARCTIC CRESCENT, May 1932

Fall is a special time at Virginia Beach for the heat and humidity are gone. Edgar had already planted flowers and was dreaming about fixing up the yard.

The place where we are now living doesn't just yet permit making much of a show for A garden, or trees, as we are very close to a little fresh water lake [308 Arctic Crescent at 14th St.]. Can you imagine looking out one window and seeing the lake, while looking out another and seeing the ocean? The drain in the back of the place is rather low at present. If I can find such a thing as the 'root of all evil' that you speak of, and cover up some of the reeds and rushes around the lake, I might have a very pretty little place.

(464-12) R23 10-21-32

We are having most glorious weather here now; in fact, we have been having all Fall. We have had one frost, but what little flowers we were able to straggle along with us as we moved so much last year are doing their level best to shed some of their beauty, and to give expression of their concept of their Maker.   O that we would all do just that, and – as we view nature – take a lesson from that we see about us, knowing that each flower, each shrub, each blade of grass as it lifts its head, is trying to express to man (who is the wayward creature of all earth) something of the glory it feels in its Maker, presenting the very best it can under whatever circumstance or environ it finds itself; raising no hullabaloo because times are hard or conditions bad, but doing the best it can with what it has.

(259) CF 11-17-32

A warm spell in January made his green thumb itch, but the new yard wasn't big enough for all the trees he wanted to plant.

We are having quite wonderful weather here at present.   It looks almost as if spring has begun, which makes me feel like getting out to scratch in the ground.   I'm beginning to plan for some little beds of flowers.   I want to get a fruit tree or two; they may never bear any fruit, but – to me – their blossoms and leaves are equally as pretty as shade trees.   The very fact that they <u>might</u> be productive makes it all the more interesting.   I can't help but feel that each plant, whether it be a tree, flower or bulb, appreciates in some way the care and attention we give it.   Although their response at times may be very discouraging, so are our attempts with many of our fellow man.

(464) CF 1-17-33

We are having some very beautiful weather here at present. It makes me feel very much like getting out and digging around in the ground, except we haven't hardly room enough to turn around – to say nothing of trying to make a few beds and planting a few seeds; though when I find time I'm going to get a tree or two. I'm one of those simpletons that believes a tree – fruit tree – is just about as pretty as any other shrub, and though I may not be able to have much fruit I would enjoy the beautiful blossoms. Of course, we had all this on the place we left at 35th Street, for we had every manner of fruit tree almost – and got fruit too! but the blooms were beautiful. When the peaches, apples, plums, cherries and pears all began to bloom, why it was pretty. I don't know if we will ever be able to make this place so we would have room enough, but if we ever do we will have a very nice little place to plant a few trees. First we must fill up a lake, for when the rains are very hard the lake fills up around the house at present. Now, if we can get something to crowd out the water, maybe it will supply something for a tree to grow.

(2457) CF 1-18-33

Although it turned cold again at the end of January, his flowers, amazingly, were still in bloom. The harsh beach weather stressed his fruit trees and made them more susceptible to insects. Although the fairies and nature spirits are very sensitive to pesticides and withdraw when they are used, Edgar seemed to be able to spray and maintain his relationship with them.

We have been having quite a nice little spell here, but this last week it has turned very cold for us (about forty) and we have had an unusually high wind. The violets in the the yard, though, are in bloom, and I have a few pinks – and what not – that have weathered the storm. In the house we have some potplants that are in bloom, begonias, hyacinths, etc. My African violets are living but, of course, not showing much signs of life as yet.

Yes, close to the seashore – and with the high winds – we often have blights to the fruit. I usually like to piddle around and spray them with something, dig around the roots, and that usually gets rid of the insects that make the fruit so faulty. If I possibly can, I do want to fix up this place and have a few trees – as I had started at the other place where we lived.   I'll try to get to work right away on a flower bed, at least.   As the adjoining lot is not in use, possibly there would be no objections to my using it for such.

(464) CF 1-28-33

He seemed to be slowly recovering from the loss of his first garden for he went back for a visit.

The flowers were beginning to show some blooms, but when the winter blew in the other day it sort of discouraged them.   So, I'm afraid it's good-bye to the violets, jonquils, pinks, and all the things that were showing their pretty faces.   It's been real cold, and the weather man promises much colder tonight.

I've been wanting to put in a tree or two.   Inasmuch as I haven't gotten the back portion fixed up yet, I can only put one or two on the side - but haven't been able to make the riffle yet.

A few days ago I was down on the 35th Street place.   The little trees there certainly looked beautiful, and they really seemed quite glad to see me.   It seems a shame to have to leave things of the kind, but possibly they will be of a service to someone.   At least, if people appreciate them in any way, I'm sure they will do their best to give their expression of life, or God.

(2457) CF 2-7-33

By the end of March and early April he was planting shrubs and fruit trees which were close to his heart, but he still missed his chickens.

Several of the Study Group in Norfolk are rather inclined to like beautiful gardens, and From time to time bring or send us some very pretty plants. A few days ago a lady came out with some beautiful little trees; pussy willow, Calycanthus, Hydrangea, snowdrop, crepe myrtle, etc. All of these, so far, seem to be doing very well. There were around the house a few little wild cherry trees, but as I have said before I am one of those that believes if you have room for anything of the kind of fruit tree – that may at some time bear fruit – will be just as pretty as anything, or as something that isn't any good at all. So I have made room for a few fruit trees. All of them haven't arrived yet, but the little peach tree I put out has a few blossoms on it already.

(464-13) R7 3-20-33

Well, a friend brought a few more trees today. So I've been out putting them around the little lake – a few willows and poplars. While the grounds are not such as to lend themselves for so much of this improvement on our own lot, we went over on the other fellow's and beautified his, which will no doubt aid ours also.

(464-13) R9 4-4-33

I certainly have missed my chickens since I've been in this place. We haven't a large enough lot (that is, that's exposed to view) to give us enough room for chickens, unless they were ducks – and then we would have to put a fence around the lake and I'm not a very good mud dauber; but who knows – maybe some day we will be differently arranged and we can have them again. I believe you aided me personally in building my first chicken coop, and also sent me quite a number of my first flock, the last of which we only got rid of when we moved here last June.

(2457) CF 4-14-33

Edgar had some challenges but made friends with the priest and intuitively knew he liked watermelons.

Well, my garden hasn't been doing as well as I would like to see it. I don't know whether it's because of my seed being planted too early, or what. Anyway, I've gotten a very poor stand; and very recently, since it has been warm (and it's a real summer here, everybody ready to go in the ocean), I started in to dig and make a vegetable – as well as flower –garden. Now I have a few beans, radishes, some corn, tomatoes, okra, squash, and a few things like that, which to me – at least – appears to be a great deal better when fresh. They are looking very good, though the ground is very dry for them. Of course, I threw in a few hills of cantaloupe and watermelon for good luck. As I told you, the Catholic Church is across the street. I met the Father [Father Philip P. Brennan] on the grounds the other day and told him I had been digging over here, and had dedicated one hill of watermelons to him. He seemed to appreciate it; said there were only a few things he could eat, but watermelon was one of them that he really enjoyed.

Our plants and shrubs are doing fairly well. I went into the market in Norfolk a few days ago and got some plants to put right close to the house; a nice little pansy bed and quite a few other things that will be coming along from time to time. We have quite a few ragged robins; I don't know whether that's the name for them or bachelor buttons; anyway, you will possibly know what I mean. All of these are looking very good, considering the weather and general conditions. But many of seed didn't come up.

Our violets have practically all gone. A few roses (that have been transplanted several times) are beginning to have some buds; in fact, we have gathered quite a few in the last week or so. I haven't enough of them, though, to make much fuss over.

(464-13) R12 5-15-33

It was not easy to start another garden in an area that was more exposed to the ocean and had wild rabbits. It also takes time to make compost and build up the soil.

I haven't as yet been able to see a great deal of returns from my little efforts with the flowers and garden.   Only a few things have done as well as we would like to see them, but that is caused - I'm sure - from the dry weather, as much as anything else – and possibly the unfertility of the soil, being so close to the ocean, with so much sand, etc.

(464) CF 6-23-33

Well I wish I had a place for some chickens, but this pond is so close to our back yard – we might have ducks instead, except it's not the kind of pond that lends itself very well to such activities; too many weeds or cattails growing in it; too much mud – and I guess the turtles would eat them up anyway. I don't suppose ducks would be so good that close to the house anyway, but when we get the pond filled up, maybe we can fix up a little place for ducks – and chickens also.   I have tried to dig up a little garden, but it hasn't done so well.   I started in most too late, and I suppose the ground is so poor – and it hasn't rained enough.   We did have some beans, but a flock of rabbits next to us thought we planted the garden especially for them, so they ate up all the beans.   I think I'll plant some potatoes - maybe that'll give the moles a chance.   We have a few flowers – nasturtiums and gladiolli, especially.   We'll do better next year, with an earlier start.

(2457) CF 6-23-33

My garden has been quite disappointing. We are so close to the ocean that when we have the hard spells and very strong winds, the vegetation is burned, I suppose from the salt spray - almost as if a real frost had swept over it. It shows so on the little trees, too, that we have been trying to grow around the place; it makes them all one-sided and blasts them on the north and east side. The flowers are looking fairly good at present; that is, what we have; plenty of nasturtiums and zinnias, these are very pretty. We have had plenty of gladioli, and I think the prospects are that we will have some very pretty cosmos. We have had a few snapdragons, but these haven't done so well. The zinnias and nasturtiums are about the prettiest things for this climate, for the time of year. The little vegetable garden, though, is blasted entirely; the salt is not so good, and then this weather has been awful. The rabbits, too, ate up my beans; and it seems now they are cultivating a taste for tomatoes. The roses haven't been so wonderful, but for very young shrubs I think they have done very nicely – considering everything.

(464-13) R16 8-10-33

Things got even worse two weeks later on August 23, 1933 when an extremely severe hurricane (David) made landfall. It broke records, for it had the highest tide - 9.69 feet above mean low water, and the lowest pressure – 28.68. The ocean came across Pacific Avenue, merged with Lake Holly, and totally flooded Edgar's garden and basement with salt water.

We are still sitting in the middle of a lake.   It was very lucky for us that the boys had come home on the 19th.   Of course, all the lights were out for several days, and we had no way of preparing anything to eat except on the little gasoline stove the boys used on their trip.   We could boil coffee and fry eggs on it, and eat bread when we could get it.   There was a greal deal of damage to the Beach, not near as much – however – as between here and Cape Henry, Ocean View, Willoughby and Norfolk; they were much harder hit than Virginia Beach. Our greatest disturbance is the water in the basement, and the "reading" office room where I'm now writing looks like an express office with a lot of trunks left on hand; as we had to pile everything out of the basement and get it somewhere out of the water. The water was about four and a half feet deep. We have no backyard; in fact, for several days we could only get into the house through one door.   The ocean broke through and it ran the lake into the back of our house.   So, until the road up above us is fixed – and I don't know how soon that will be – we'll still be sitting in the lake.

(254-66) R4 8-28-33

He had apparently been able to find room for some chickens again, for they were inundated.

…There was a great deal of property damage here, but no lives lost. With US, however, We don't know just where we are AT, yet, as we are still in the lake. You remember the small lake in back of us? Well, there's quite a large one now; in fact, VERY large! We can get out of the house through one door, if we can jump; otherwise we have to be paddled or carried on somebody's back.
…I believe it's begun to rain again. It has rained so much that some chickens I had in the coop have turned to ducks. Good swimmers! Had to be!

(2733-3) R16 8-29-33

Mrs. (464) wondered if he had survived and Edgar replied:

…We had quite a blow.   There was not as much damage in Virginia Beach proper As farther up the coast along Chesapeake Bay.   The sea wall here, which extends nearly three miles, I'm sure prevented much more damage; for, above the sea wall, where the ocean broke through, there was a great deal of property damage, though no lives lost.   As for ourselves, I believe I have told you that we live right on a lake. It <u>was</u> a fresh water lake, but the ocean broke through and filled our little basin with salt water. Our basement was five feet deep in water, but it didn't get into the house proper.   The work I recently did in the basement probably has prevented an undermining of the foundations.   The water is gradually receding, but it makes a mess around the place.   Of course our garden is gone, and the flowers, as the water covered everything in the yard. It was especially pitiful to see our watermelon patch floating out in the lake. But I'm glad it was no worse than it was.
    We have had rather a strenuous summer here, with quite a bit of very unusual weather; and then the season ending with such a storm has been quite hard on many of those who live during the winter on what they make during the summer months here.

(464) CF 9-7-33

Gardeners know anything can happen, never become discouraged for long, and always hope that next year will be better. Which it was, and Father Brennan gave him some roses.

During those days when the ground was somewhat in order before the last rainy spell I had the opportunity to dig a little in the ground around here. I have gotten a little piece of garden started and a few spots with some flowers that I hope will be coming on after a bit. The garden is beginning to show some signs as I notice the radishes and beans coming up already.

Such days as these certainly makes for the d esire to be outside. Owing to the high water we found it was necessary to move the bed of bulbs we tried to have. This, of course, will make most of those quite late, but I am in hopes that we can get them in yet. I am having to wait, though, a few days now, until the ground is dry enough to put them in. Tried this morning, but they don't go much.

The Catholic priest who lives just across the street from us has been very lovely. He sent over some rose bushes a week or so ago which fills out a row of roses that should come along by the middle of the summer, anyway.

(464) CF 5-7-34

Had the chance to get my little scrap of a garden worked out and then there came a good rain on it and it looks very good.   I don't know just how well it will work out.

…I am sure you missed the opportunity you had to go out and pick violets.   I think they, possibly, with pansies, are the most beautiful of the spring flowers.   Of course, nothing scarcely compares with roses.

…We have quite a bit of clay right around us here, but it seems to be of such a nature that it requires mixing either would [wood] mold or stable manure with it to make it any good.   The iris here are blooming very good.   I haven't a great many, but they are gradually getting a start.   I had quite a lot at some of the other places, but moving them so much and breaking them up hasn't been so good.

…I have a little patch of pinks – spice pinks, I suppose.   This is the first time they have bloomed since I have been here.   Not a great many on it as yet, but they are the most fragrant things I have ever seen.   Even days after they were picked they give off a lovely odor.

…The fox gloves and delphiniums are very beautiful when we get farther back from the ocean than we are here at the Beach.   I have seen some very beautiful beds of them.   I would love to be able to have such.   My nicotine hasn't started as yet, but if it is anything like you describe it will no doubt give us a great deal to think about as time goes on.

(464) CF 5-19-34

IRIS

We, too, have had quite a spell of very dry weather.   Recently, though, we had a very good rain and it has freshened things up a bit.   I have a little vegetable garden – just a few beans, squash, Okra, tomatoes, and such.   The beans suffered a great deal from the drouth.   In fact, at first we had abundance, enough to give away.   I went out, though, this morning, expecting to be able to gather possibly enough for one meal, but – nothing doing!   Plenty of blooms, however, and they look as if they might in another week have plenty more.   The okra is fine – so are the tomatoes.   Of course, the beets, radishes and onions are practically all gone. May have a few more a little later on.

The flowers, though, have done beautifully.   Of course, our principal ones are Nasturtiams and Zinnias.   Certainly keeps one busy for a few hours every day trying to keep them so that they wont spoil.   They are very beautiful.   I am in hopes the showers have come in time for you and your garden for it to be all right.

(464) CF 7-13-34

Three years after moving in, his garden supplied him with everything he needed except four staples from the grocery store. Not too bad for self-sufficiency in spite of battling the weather and dry spells.

...been very dry here garden about to ruin, trying to rain today but hasnt done much at as yet do hope we will have a good soaking rain before it quits, need it have plenty of beans, Tomatoes, Okra Beets Squash, radishes peppers carrots.so if it rains will be fine for us Onions also.so a little bread and meat occasionaly sugar and coffee.is aboyt all we need.

(340) CF 7-8-35

Gardens need constant attention. The grass and weeds take over whenever they can, especially if there is no mulch and the gardner has been travelling.

...just came back from a little better than three weeks stay in N.Y. very nice trip,met lots of people,but too much of a city for me,am too much country, glad to get back,and then too my garden and flowers were suffering for attention,as the house was practically closed up,no one to look after things and the suffered,well havent any scarce as yet for those that were to be planted have just gotten in the ground garden and flowers,and until we have rain wont be coming up either,but hope for the best.Iris,Roses,Violets Pinks,and such are fine look pretty good since have gotten the grass and weed away from th m.

(464) CF 5-13-36

In July he had a vision while working in the garden.

I was in the garden here at work when I heard a noise like the noise of a swarm of bees. When I looked to see where they were, I saw that the noise came from a chariot in the air with 4 white horses and a driver. I did not see the face of the driver. The experience lasted only a few minutes. I was trying to persuade myself that it was not true, that it was only imagination, when I heard a voice saying, "Look behind you." I looked and beheld a man in armor, with a shield, a helmet, knee guards, a cape but no weapon of any kind. His countenance was like the light; his armor was as silver or aluminum.

He raised his hand in salute and said, "The chariot of the Lord and the horsemen thereof." Then he disappeared. I was really weak, not from fright but from awe and wonder.

...It was a most beautiful experience and I hope I may be worthy of many more.

(294-185) T

His guidance explained that when he did not receive a kind word, a smile, or encouraging words from a friend, he would feel that something was wrong. He was to remember that the armor of the Lord is a defense against temptation, and that His chariot would take wings to make Edgar know that His promises abide when trials of every sort would come upon him and his fellow man. Pearl Harbor was just five years away.

Although things had gotten off to a rocky start, by 1937 the weather was kinder and the fairies had been busy. Edgar had a magical eye with the camera and captured the joy of Gladys' nephew (T.J. Davis) as a toddler as he danced (with the fairies?) and picked some flowers.

FLOWER BEDS SEPTEMBER 2, 1937

In 2008, T.J. shared that as a child, most of the time he loved being right in the middle of the flowers, but occasionally the bees, waving asparagus fronds or pesky fairies would scare him.

When he was older, he preferred fishing with Edgar rather than helping him 'work' in his garden. They played an aura game to decide: if T.J. could see the right colors, they would go fishing. If not, they went to the garden. One day Edgar asked him if he wanted to see the fairies. They were fast and quick like bugs, and could be seen through like gossamer. When they flew, they made musical sounds that made him feel happy or sad, and he heard them before they could be seen. One fairy that T.J. named Picasso, knew he was afraid and bothered him like a mosquito, so Edgar gave him a water gun for protection. The garden started out well in the spring of 1938; then nature dealt a cruel blow.

My garden has done very well guess considering the weather-have lots of flowers-of course the Iris have about gone here-but I moved mine this year-and they didnt have just the start they should have had posibly will be fine next year-but they had multiplied so had to move them. Tulips and Hyacinths were lovely- Roses now are very pretty-and the Delphinium is lovely remember had a bed close to house-it is very very pretty-andMo.primrose is very lovely

Vegetables have done very nicely-planted a few strawberries this year-and while nothing to speak of-to go out and gather a quart as this morning is nice-to me have had Peas,Lettuce,Raddish,Onions from my own garden all can use-that is nice and gives me something to piddle with now and then-planted me an Asparagus bed but didnt cut it this year-but looks as if it might be just fine.

Hope the weather is nice enought for you to get out-and the air

realy do you good does one good to see green fields-and things growing-o r does me good any way

(464) CF 5-17-38

We have had a very bad spell of weather here all my flowers and garden has been ruined by the salt blast and cold-look most as if frost had hit it all posibly will grow out of it as has turned warm in last day or so and will look better possibly never just the same-but posibly we will appreciate them more-

(464) CF 6-2-38

No matter what happened, Edgar could usually see the bright side and "had hopes", but one year when his crop of early tomatoes failed, he took it personally - which was unlike him.

My flowers-and garden-is about a failure this year-early ones were fine but the cold spell killed most of my flowering shrubbery-guess cant have sea breeze and shrubbery also-and the garden-well just a few things-but when havent any tomatoes feel as if am complete failure-and couldnt get them to live this year some way.

(464) CF 7-4-38

Think will have raspberries next year-just put mine out this spring My tomatoes did not turn out so well this year-that is early ones just have them coming along now-and that is late for them here-have never tried so much in them but the recipe you gave me last year was fine and we all enjoyed that too.

...My flowers are gradually begining to fade-tho still have some very pretty ones In the yard-the garden isnt so much-but still have Okra-Beans-Cabbage-beets and tomatoes are just about plentiful now.

(464) CF 8-18-38

Around Christmastime his narcissus was blooming!

Thank goodness weather here has been very nice-some very cool weather fr ezing of mornings and like but has been lovely here for some time,Christmas day I gathered som narcissus out of the yard and the Poinsetters and Christmas cactus are beautiful on the front poarch.

(464) CF 1-3-39

He expanded the side yard, and built a bird house and a hutch for a pet rabbit a friend gave him.

> ...rabbit is fine-the bird has lain two eggs will posibly be setting by the time you are home, or maybe hatching- have transplanted roses-and hope to finish soon the filling of the side of the yard-took up posts on side also and have them in back now-looks much better-
>
> (487) CF 3-6-39

RABBIT HUTCH, [1942]
T.J. Davis age 7

In November, he was telling Mrs. (464) about his sons' green thumbs (or lack of one), and giving her more nature advice.

> Have lots of fall flowers now-while have had a bit of frost not enough to kill them all. some very pretty roses even as yet.
> A friend gave me some plants a few days ago-most of them flowering shrubs have put them out and hope they live-seems they live much better for some people than for others-for instance the younger boy any thing he plants seems to do well. while the older dosnt seem able to make any thing live. Plants are fond of you and grow for you that is why they do so well-and know you cant fool nature,so there is no use your saying at times you are so terrible

about things. nature proves what you are.

(464) CF 11-14-39

In the spring of 1941, his garden and fruit trees weren't doing very well in a drought.

Has been very pleasant weather here-only fearfully dry-hasnt rained on my garden to get it wet since planted it,so little or nothing has come up,do have a few roses but too dry for any of the other flowers to look like any thing at all.

Guess am too close to the ocean for fruit trees to do much good-do try to have some but not much good have a Pear-Peach and Apple they are alive is about all tho did have one peach that did nicely last year-gathered about bushel or more peaches from it,but had to move that tree when built the new offices,so rest are too small for any thing as yet-if they stand the drouth may have some next year

(464) CF 5-26-41

My garden is a complete failure this year am afraid-havent had more than just enough rain to keep it alive,not enough to make any thing realy grow except grass, that comes it seems at the lest provication.tomatoes do look fairly well but beans, beets,onions,carrots and the like. well just about half what they should be.Squash-melons,okra and like,just didnt come up and hasnt been enough rain to make replanting do any thing.

You -am afraid will have to go slow on the work in garden-take it easy-go often but dont stay long at time,find I have to do that for myself.

(464) CF 6-14-41

By July the drought had broken and the garden was thriving again. But now Edgar was going to lose it because he planted on someone else's land.

Hope the change is fine for all,but am sure you will miss the garden seems we are to have a house built next to us-so good bye to my little garden which has been a real pleasure to me,with the vegetables and the like-gathered 45 delicious cantelopes from same yesterday,even with the plot laid out.and tomatoes just lots

135

of them besides the flowers. but all comes with changes that seem to come to us all.

(1770) CF 8-23-41

Edgar's niece visited for a month in August and went home with some gardenia cuttings. He told her to root them the same way her mother did roses: make a hole in a potato (sometimes it was done with a knitting needle), put a cutting in the hole and plant it in some dirt under a jar.

Glad you got the flowers home in good shape-did you try and root one of them can be done put it in dirt under a jar-in a potato like your mother does roses is the best way.

(421) CF 8-7-41

In the spring of 1942, ten years after moving in, he was finally able to acquire land next door, have a large garden, plant more fruit trees and have more of a "farm".

MORE LAND

He wrote Edgar Evans who seemed to have inherited some of Edgar's special way with plants.

Been bad weather here for several days,looks better last day or so my trees have come wish had you here to plant them am sure they

would grow-will have to get you to give them a touch when you are down.

(294) CF 3-31-42

A week later he put in a strawberry bed all by himself and paid dearly for it.

…spring here and fishing is good and as can't get help, work on grounds, yard and garden are hard – just put in a big Strawberry bed. Hope it rains but looks as if it might blow away now with out any – maybe can get used to working again, but make my old bones a bit stiff.

(2441-3) R16 4-9-42

…With regular work as well as trying to put in a bit of a garden, and guess have gotten to that age [64] where can't take it as it about put me abed, have been under the weather for last three four days.

(487) CF 4-22-42

Six days later, he bounced back, planted twice as much as usual and even thought about what he would put in the lots next door.

No rain as yet so there isnt any thing coming up in garden as yet but all looks pretty nice if and when we have a bit of rain,think seed were put in when ground was in fair shape so should be alright-tho may have to replant much of it.
   lots next to us will look nice when clened off-have man working on it and looks much better think will try and plant something there this year put in some things yesterday cabbage and like,

(487) CF 4-28-42

…had good rain Sat afternoon just after got the last of garden planted-have better than twice as much as we usualy have,hope it makes good and we can make it of use to selves and others Strawberries that planted few weeks ago are in bloom-wont be many but will have few believe.this rain should make every thing grow. little orchard looks   ood to this morning,little shouts putting out-reminds me of Grand-pa.

(243) CF 5-4-42

Is lovely here, just got my garden all in and had a very very fine rain Sat. afternoon so hope will make the garden grow – noticed this morning some of my roses seem ready to bloom. Do like to see things grow, all nature seems to me to speak so of GOD.

(2454-2) R9 5-4-42

By June he had not only been able to enlarge the garden but planted an orchard. Even though his trees had not always done well by the ocean, he was always optimistic.

Have had a busy spring. A friend was good enough to make it possible for us to have the lot and half next door to us toward the ocean – then, Miss Gladys has the next lot and ½. She intended building but the Gov. orders got a head of her, so have been cleaning this ground off and in the rear along the lake have enlarged garden and planted an orchard. Do love to see things growing and will some day be a real pretty place, I think. Garden is looking nice now –

while a bit late – is coming along and my roses are lovelier than ever this year – that has kept me on the go and a bit strenuous for the old man!

(1770-6) R1 5-19-42

By the middle of July the garden was almost gone and there weren't a lot of vegetables for soup stock.

Hot and dry here garden has about dried up-afraid wont have much soup stock this year-too much to buy the stuff to put in such but certainly makes a nice thing to have on hand-and is a whole meal in its self.

(2635) CF 7-13-42

In January and February he was thinking about the garden and still wanting chickens.

Almost envy you your hens-always enjoyed fooling with chicks havent had any since lived here have no place for them-since have a bit of land wanted to build a hen house but the folks here almost forbid it-garden is then my out let,nice to prepare ground now for next spring-hope have a nice garden and do well with it.

(585) CF 1-13-43

Was fine weather here for few days xxx so began on the garden put a few thing into the ground things they say are alright,as the ground was right,but this morning there is snow on them,maybe it will keep them warm and in shape to be alright if and when the weather gets better, hope to have a real garden if possible,tho not cheap work cost 50 cents per hour,but will feel am doing better myself if and when can give a few hours work out there.

(487) CF 2-27-43

Edgar's biography, There Is A River by Tom Sugrue, was published March, 1943. It made him an instant celebrity that brought mixed blessings. People called him all hours of the day and night and began showing up on his doorstep without an appointment. They took time away from his garden, fishing and correspondence which kept him centered, balanced and rejuvenated. He had not realized how much of an impact the book would have on his life and health, and the stress shows in this picture taken next to one of his rosebushes in the spring of 1943.

Both sons had been drafted overseas and help was scarce.

...been wet for last few days,makes grass grow,and am out of yard help,as they are paying now my man Friday 1.25 an hour to dig ditches,and cant quite meet that for some one to work garden and mow the lawn,dont quite know what will do,got behind with

letters by going out yesterday and gathering strawberries,took Sally [Hugh Lynn's wife] some and carried a big pan of them up to Kat [Edgar Evans wife] this morning,she and her Mother had gone to town but we left them there. have a lot of peas right for canning,soon as can get into the garden.

(487) CF 5-25-43

Although he had gotten more land for a garden, he didn't have the time or energy for it.

...the rain and hot weather the grass has run away with garden-but simply cant do it myself even if the grass and weeds do take it-like to played myself out just gathering peas.so dont know what will do-did get man to cut yard,but it was so high was a job, and dosnt look so good either-but hate to see all that work and money in garden and then lose it.

(341) CF 6-3-43

Edgar Evans was stationed near a lake and had more time to go fishing than Edgar.

So you got one of the fish-that size must have been nice havent been able to get to the pier scarcely for the last eight weeks-was out a while yesterday,but nothing doing,did get a nice bass the last time did try-and two of the largest cat-fish have ever caught out there.

Black berries are just beginning to get ripe,will try and get a few put up if possible, do hope to get some soup stock this year if possible but have so little time,hope tho to get some one to help with letters if so can have a bit more time. for such things have a nice lot of beans,squash,onions beets and Carrots just now,garden looks wrather grassy for mine but havent been able to do it myself nor have much help,

(294) CF 6-27-43

During World War II the government asked people to plant a "victory" garden and can the harvest to help with the war effort, but Edgar had always done that.

I haven't been able to do very much with the garden this year. I started out with the idea of really having a Victory garden and putting up some vegetables, but the man who was helping me got a Government job and I got so busy that the grass is knee-high all over it.   I would put up some vegetable soup; that, I am very fond of. I put up a few berries and that is about all. Well, we manage to get along--don't have much to eat, but we have so much to be thankful for.

(464) CF 7-15-43

By the end of July, he had managed to make his soup stock but the garden was becoming a lawn.

the grass has taken the garden but started out this year to have some Soup stock and have enough to have soup once a week for five months,so that isnt bad for such a bad year for me,yard looks better got a man to cut it today,has to do the hedge tho,but the rain makes the grass in lawn look nice. hedge is coming alright,-

(294) CF 7-22-43

EDGARS' HEDGE

Mailbags of letters requesting readings began arriving from all over the country. Edgar was giving six and seven readings a day instead of two that his guidance had advised, and was exhausted.

It is quite nice of you to suggest such a dedication of the book, but I am sure that I much preferred it had not been done. Too many nice things are being said about me. Too many people are becoming too dependent on me. I do not know as I am able to take it.

(1472-1) R19 8-20-43

By the spring of 1944, he was so overwhelmed he couldn't even plant a garden or write his garden pen-pal.

No, it has been such bad weather I don't suppose anyone has gotten in much of a garden as yet. I haven't even undertaken anything and don't suppose I can. Help is so uncertain, and yet we are possibly in better position to undertake it than at any time since we have been here, if we had the help. I hardly know which way to go; have too many things to think about.

(2072-1) R3 4-5-44

Haven't undertaken to do any gardening this year, in fact, it has been so wet, and is raining today.   Couldn't have done it, if I had wanted to, but I had such a sad experience with it last year when I tried to put in so much for a victory garden and it was all ruined, so there will be very little, if anything, that I try to plant this year. The place looks fairly well; pretty ragged in many ways, but when we get this lot on the west side all cleared up and settled, it will make it a very good looking place.

(487) CF 4-27-44

Haven't done much with garden made such a mess of it last year didn't try for just can't look after it.
(2441-4) R28 5-16-44

In August, he told Hugh Lynn that he was more than a year behind with appointments, was not sleeping well, and had to take it slow because his heart was enlarged. A few weeks later he had a stroke, and the last reading he ever gave was for himself on September 17, 1944 which suggested that he go to Roanoke until he was "well or dead". While away, his thoughts were still with garden, however, for he had finally been able to hire a temporary gardener by the name of Baynes. He asked Gertrude to telephone Gladys with instructions for him to dig a trench by the side of the office and plant tulip bulbs.

Tell Baynes I dig up the bulbs every fall and plant fresh.   Dig a trench about 6 inches deep, put a little sand in bottom, then a little fertilizer, and then cover 8 to 10 inches.

(294) CF 10-12-4

T. J. DAVIS by EDGAR'S TULIPS

At the end of November, Edgar Evans was given military leave to bring him home to Virginia Beach. On January 3, 1945, Edgar Cayce passed away. He was laid to rest in the family burial ground in Riverside Cemetery, Hopkinsville, Kentucky, with a simple gravestone next to his beloved flowers and fairies.

The following April, "...the peach and pear tree in the yard began to bloom, and the bulbs that Bains [Baynes] planted opened their petals."1

ENDNOTES

1-Kirkpatrick p. 523

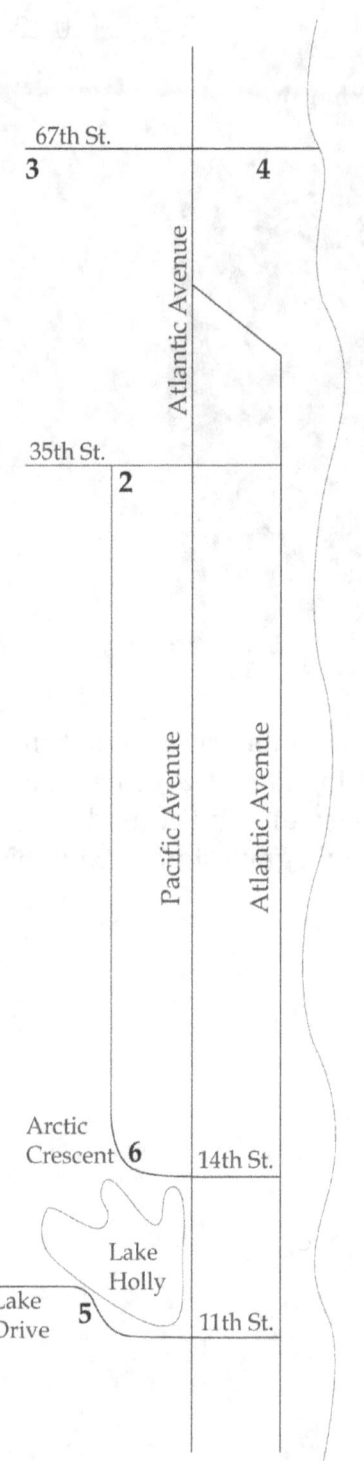

2 – SECOND GARDEN
September 1925 – May 1931
115 West 35th St. (now 315
Arctic)

3 – THRID GARDEN
June 1928 – February 1931
Cayce Hospital 105th St. and
Atlantic Avenue (now A.R.E. –
215 67th St.)

4 – FOURTH GARDEN
June 1931 – February 1932
105th St. and Oceanfront (now
6610 67th St.)

5 – FIFTH GARDEN
March 1932 – April 1932
403 Lake Drive – Pinewood
section, 11th St. extended

6 – SIXTH GARDEN
May 1932 – January 1945
308 Arctic Crescent (torn down
1976)

Chapter Ten

IN EDGAR'S MEMORY

Samuel A. Harris D.D.S., a member and friend of A.R.E., gave a gift of $75,000 in 1993 to expand the existing meditation garden located on the west side of the Visitors Center. In an interview in Venture Inward (bi-monthly A.R.E. magazine), he shared what motivated him.

"I remember the first time I sat in that garden. I was attending a conference. It was pleasant just *sitting*. It's really one of the best places I've ever been. I can't describe the feeling I have when I'm there. I thought, if this place makes me feel this way, what could it do for others? So, three years ago, sitting here, I decided I wanted to give a little something back. You can lose yourself in that garden. It's going to be a real breath-taker when everything grows up."

It was dedicated October 1997, and is a living memorial to Edgar's love of nature. In 2006, a labyrinth was built in front of the hospital building with a fountain on the same spot where Edgar had built one for his mother. Photographs courtesy of Andy Russo, age 15.

HARRIS PRAYER AND MEDITATION GARDEN, July 2008

FOUNTAIN, July 2008

Although not planted by Edgar, his favorite flower - the rose - still grows at A.R.E. in four places. Photographs by the author.

TERRACE FACING EAST, May 2009
Hybrid Rose

"The Fairy" rose (bred in England in 1931), thrives in a three foot high by thirty foot long hedge next to the plum trees. The flower fades to almost white as it ages, and is one of the best summer blooming varieties that tolerates poor soil and neglect.

SOUTH SIDE BY THE DRIVEWAY, June 2009
"The Fairy" Rose

DAY SPA , May 2009
Knock Out Rose

VISITOR CENTER/LIBRARY ENTRANCE, November 2008
Knock Out Rose

REFLECT UPON THESE THINGS
GOD IN NATURE

(Q) What books should the body read at this time?
(A) Nature is the best book of all! (903-6) T

~

For the love of nature grows, and is akin to God. For all nature manifests life, and life IS the manifestation of God. (1968-1) T

~

...for, as was given of old, "Be thou fruitful and multiply; subdue the earth and that therein". It didn't say abuse the earth or that therein, nor use for thine own aggrandizement; for only that that may be personally used from day to day is necessary. (520-2) T

~

Keep the interests, of course, in nature, and in nature's storehouse. Keep close to the earth oft; with the feet well on the ground, but look to the mountain. For the mount is the hill of God. (2830-2) T

~

Have more and more of nature and of God's outdoors...For each blade of grass, each blossom, each tree, each crag, each mountain, each river, each lake is as a gift from the Creative Forces in man's experience that he may know more of the love of God. (1248-1) T

~

Think not that the snail or the dragon fly, as he crawls from his slime, does not glorify his Maker. And as he mounts on his wings of gossamer, he fills that place for which he has been - in his realm of activity - designated; in his field, his manner of showing forth his love as manifested from the Creator in the materialized world. (254-68) T

Go to the ant, thou sluggard, - understand his ways and be wise! Remember, of course, the song of the grasshopper, as well as the ant or the bee, - but know in Whom ye have believed. For He, the Giver of all good and perfect gifts, has given these - the handiwork of His creation - as a pattern or example or lesson, that ye - too - may learn. They choose by their instinct. (1965-1) T

~

Before this we find the entity was in the land of the present nativity, among those Native peoples called the Indians, yet those who worshiped nature – as it were – and the activities of same as they influence man or the children of man, by the very activity of water in its fall from the clouds as well as those expressions in the spring and the rill and the river, - as well as the songs of the birds and of nature and of the natural things that made for not merely convenience but that give in the deeper expression the insight as to the love the gracious Father manifests to the children of men, in giving that ensample in which the study of same may be seen how that he who understands nature walks close with God. (1904-2) T

~

The entity should keep close to all of those things that have to do with outdoor activities, for it is the best way to keep yourself young - to stay close to nature, close to those activities in every form of exercise that breathes in the deep ozone and the beauty of nature. For you may breathe it into thine own soul, as you would a sunset or a morning sun rising. And see that sometimes - it's as pretty as the sunset! (3374-1) T

~

Spiritualize the ideals; that is, as the entity sees in the emotions in relationships with others, let them find expression in the visions that might be expressed in nature, in the activities of nature, the unfolding of the bud, the motherhood of the bird, the strength of the storm, the powers and beauty of the sea, any of that in nature. The outlines and symmetrical beauty of an orange, an apple, a lily, a tree, yea a vine as it may cling. (3664-1) T

~

For, as seen, each animal, each bird, each fowl, has been so named for some peculiarity of that individual beast, bird or fowl, and in this manner represents some particular phase of man's development in the earth's plane, or that consciousness of some particular element or personality that is manifested in man. (294-87) T

~

For Life as it manifests, whether in the grass, the rose, the tree, the dog, the cat, the bird, the animal, IS a manifestation of that ye worship as God. (1367-1) T

~

Keep – KEEP – the heart singing. Look deeper into the heart of the rose. LISTEN to the song of the bird. See the paintings of His face in the setting and the rising sun. See the loveliness in the moonbeam that turns all into the radiance of His glory. See in the raindrop, the storm, all nature, and even in those ugly things in peoples lives, the desire for expression rather than the hate and the turmoil and the disorders. (410-2) T

~

Then who may tell the rose where or when to bloom? For it takes from whatever may be its surroundings, and when encompassed even by man it does the best possible to be the beauty, the joy, and to give out that which is pleasing in the service to God. Thy whole lesson is in that. (2778-2) T

~

No one mind may conceive all that may be done through the power of the Master Musician; for it may bud as the rose, it may be the song of the frog, - or of any – even those that would be to SELF as those that would be GRATING vibrations; for the cricket on the hearth to self is obnoxious! but to some would bring harmony and peace, as home! (281-8) T

~

The song of the bird, the beauty of the rose, the buzz of the bee, the activities of those things that give forth in themselves the expressions of the joy of just using – for the time being – a portion of God in their activity. Would that all men everywhere could gain but that consciousness in life and life's experience,… (410-2) T

~

Is the oak the lord over the vine? Is the Jimson beset before the tomato? Are the grassy roots ashamed of their flower beside the rose?

All those forces in nature are fulfilling rather those purposes to which their Maker, their Creator, has called them into being. (1391-1) T

~

Have more and know more of nature and of God's outdoors, rather than man's. See nature not "in the rough," then; rather in the expressions of Life! For each blade of grass, each blossom, each tree, each crag, each mountain, each river, each lake is as a gift from the Creative Forces in man's experience that he may know more of the love of God. (1248-1) T

~

(Q) A move to the country is contemplated
(A) (Interrupting) By all means, move; for the closer associations with nature, nature's storehouse, and to the God of nature that is within and may manifest in self, will bring an awakening. (2986-1) T

~

A final thought from Edgar expressed in a letter to Mrs. (1770) on January 12, 1940:

Every one speaks of the lovely trees there in Cal. They must be beautiful for am all ways reminded of that line when see a lovely tree - "only God can make a tree."

EDGAR WITH HIS TREES
SEASHORE STATE PARK

RESOURCE GUIDE

KEY: T – Text document (Reading)
      B – Background document
      R – Report document
      CF – Correspondence File
      D – Edgar's Diary
      P – Photographs

T – TEXT DOCUMENT (READING)
Gladys Davis created an indexing system for the readings to protect the identity of each individual. The first set of numbers represent a person's name. The number after the dash tells the sequential number in which the reading was given. For example: (2072-1) T is the first reading, and (2072-10) T is the tenth reading.

The public may view copies of the actual Edgar Cayce readings at the Association for Research and Enlightenment (A.R.E.) Library. A computerized version is available as a membership benefit at www.edgarcayce.org

B – BACKGROUND
Any background information (personal information, how they found Edgar Cayce, current health problems, questions to be asked) is given before a reading. For example: (1005-1) B2 8-8-24. B2 is the second section written August 8, 1924.

R - REPORTS
Follow-up correspondence is found after a reading under Reports. For example: (2072-3) R6 3-10-43. R6 is the sixth section written March 10, 1943.

CF – CORRESPONDENCE FILE
Letters that may not have been made public are stored in the ECF archives in Gladys Davis' general correspondence file. For example: (294) CF 4-30-39.

D – Edgar's diary entries are from March 18 to May 20, 1938.

P – PHOTOGRAPHS
Copies of photographs are from the ECF archival collection.

BIBLIOGRAPHY

Adams, Denise Wiles. *Restoring American Gardens*. Portland, OR. Timber Press, 2004

Andrews, Ted. *Animal Speak*. Woodbury, MN. Llewellyn Publications, 1993

Andrews, Ted. *Enchantment of the Faerie Realm*. Woodbury, MN. Llewellyn Publications, 1993

Andrews, Ted. *Nature Speak*. Jackson, TN. Dragonhook Publishing, 2004

Ballard, Juliet Brooke. *Treasures from Earth's Storehouse*. Virginia Beach, VA. ARE Press, 1980

Bro, Harmon. *A Seer Out of Season*. New York, NY. Penguin Books, 1989

Clark, Glenn. *The Man Who Talks With the Flowers*. St Paul, MN. Macalester Park Publishing Co, 1939

Colton, Ann Ree. *Watch Your Dreams*. Glendale, CA. ARC Publishing Co., 1973

Duggan, Sandra. *Edgar Cayce's Guide to Colon Care*. Weymouth MA. Inner Vision Publishing, 1995

Frejer, B. Ernest. *The Edgar Cayce Companion*. Virginia Beach, VA. ARE Press, 1995

Gabbay, Simone RN, C/P. *Nourishing the Body Temple*. Virginia Beach, VA. ARE Press, 1999

Grieve, Mrs. M. *A Modern Herbal, Vol. II I-Z*. New York, NY. Dover Publications, 1971

Gurudas. *The Spiritual Properties of Herbs*. San Rafael, CA. Cassandra Press, 1988

Jarvis, D.C., MD. *Folk Medicine*. New York, NY. Henry Holt & Co., 1958

Jensen, Dr. Bernard. *Foods That Heal*. Garden City Park, NY. Avery Publishing Group, 1988

Kirkpatrick, Sidney D. *Edgar Cayce an American Prophet*. New York, NY. Penguin Publications, 2000

Reilly, Harold J. and Brod, Ruth Hagy. *The Edgar Cayce Handbook for Health Through Drugless Therapy*. Virginia Beach, VA. ARE Press, 1975

Scott, Cyril. *The Boy Who Saw True*. Essex, England. The CW Daniel Company Limited, 1953

Smith, A. Robert. *About My Father's Business*. Norfolk, VA. The Donning Company, 1988

Smith, A. Robert. *The Lost Memoirs Of Edgar Cayce*. Virginia Beach, VA. ARE Press, 1997

Sugrue, Thomas. *There Is a River*. Virginia Beach, VA. ARE Press, 1943

Thomas, Jeanette M. *The Edgar Cayce Plant Encyclopedia, Volume One*. UK Ltd. AuthorHouseTM, 2009

Tolle, Eckhart. *A New Earth*. New York, NY. Penguin Group (USA) Inc., 2005

Tompkins, Peter. *Secrets of the Soil*. New York, NY. Harper & Row, 1989

Tompkins, Peter. *The Secret Life of Nature*. New York, NY. Harper-Collins, 1997

Virtue, Doreen. *Fairies 101*. Carlsbad, CA. Hay House, 2007

Virtue, Doreen. *Healing With the Fairies*. Carlsbad, CA. Hay House, 2001

CONTACT A.R.E.

For further information about Edgar Cayce's
Association for Research and Enlightenment, Inc., (A.R.E.)

please write:
A.R.E.
215 67th Street
Virginia Beach, VA 23451

or call:
1-800-333-4499
1-757-428-3588

or visit the website:
www.edgarcayce.org

www.ingramcontent.com/pod-product-compliance
Lightning Source LLC
Chambersburg PA
CBHW081103290526
45795CB00006B/1971

* 9 7 8 1 5 1 4 2 8 4 9 9 5 *